FINDING PURPOSE

Steven Mitchell, Adriana Soto,

April Peebles, Johnathan Kendrick,

Rob O'Brien, Catherine Frenes, Mary Tilton

Island Creek Publishing

Copyright © 2019 by Island Creek Publishing

Norwalk, CA 90650

United States of America

Foreword

What is purpose? There are a number of ways that a person could try to answer this question.

Think about it this way: what is **your** purpose?

What if we were sitting in a room with each other, and I asked you that very question? How would you answer? If you responded by telling me a number of obscure details about you, such as "well, I'm good at math, so my dad says I should be an accountant, but I've also always wanted to be a rock musician...," or, "I'm good at writing, for one, so I probably should be a teacher," or "people think I'm funny, so sometimes I think that I should be a comedian...," then I would have to tell you that you are just listing some of your characteristics, traits, and personal interests, but that you have not yet begun to answer what you feel your purpose is.

Whether you know it or not, this question has probably kept you awake at night. We call it many different things - destiny, what you're here to do, the meaning of life, the universe - but what we are really talking about is purpose.

This is the thing that you feel you were made to do and were put here on the Earth to accomplish. It's the thing that you would gladly do for free, but realize that you could profit greatly if you can make it as your full-time profession. It's the thing that no matter how far you may stray away, you always find yourself coming right back to it and making it the central focus of your life. It's the talent that you seem to have always had a knack for, even when you were a kid. It's also the thing that seems so hard for everyone else to accomplish but seems to come extremely easy to you. In essence, your purpose is likely linked directly with whatever you are exceptionally talented in that also happens to come very easy to you, especially when compared to other people that you come across throughout your life's adventures.

So, what if you don't exactly know what your purpose is? If you can't say what your purpose for being here is, then how can you play the role that you are supposed to occupy in life? And more importantly, how will you know whether you are headed in the right direction, and will eventually end up in a position of happiness and success? If you don't know how to handle your purpose, then how will you make sure that you don't waste all of your time on the wrong things, instead of being the most productive when it comes to securing your version of "happily ever after?"

These are the kinds of questions that have inspired *Finding Purpose*, the very book that you are reading right now. Everyone might not talk about it, but purpose is one of the most important elements of everyone's lives, whether they are aware of it or not. This book was written to help you not only become much more aware of your life's true purpose, but it will give you a system that you can depend on to fine-tune how well you are able to realize your true purpose and enjoy a life of health, wealth, and happiness from being able to do so. Here's to you and your sacred journey of *Finding Purpose*.

PREFACE

Finding Purpose is a book written by Steven C. Mitchell, along with April Peebles, Catherine Frenes, Johnathan Kendrick, Rob O'Brien, Mary Tilton, and Andriana Soto. This group of authors, speakers, business owners/professionals, decided to share their experiences, related to finding and living in purpose.

Each of the authors explain their challenges, and unique journeys with encountering purpose, and how they were able to face those challenges for success. Purpose is an ordinary topic that people often ponder. Anyone who reads this book will receive several unique perspectives on identifying purpose, and how they can explore implementing it into their everyday lives.

There is purpose within our relationships, our careers, our education, our hobbies, our gifts, and more. It is something that can technically be neglected, but the impact of neglecting our purpose could be negatively heavy.

Our goal is for you to be inspired, whether you are living in your purpose, or searching for purpose, to deepen your connection to it, so that it may elevate various areas of your life.

Canvas

A painting is a creation from thoughts that are rare, by an artist, with strokes and dots and splashes and time and trials and mountains and clouds. And trees and oceans and frowns and smiles. But a canvas, simply sitting on walls, with no brushes and paint sitting in buckets, has no true value at all. We live a life that's filled with purpose. At times we fall with tears that hurt us. But imagine if we became our unrivaled selves, and we kept on rising, even as we fell. And lost the fears of losing some. We have grounds and skies and moons and suns. We're not just a canvas. But a creation of beauty of errored perfection, a life that is layered with pleasure and lessons. We are colors and shades with textures and tones and voices that rage through megaphones. Expressed by waves, hitting the shore and this is why we are more than just a canvas.

Paintings...

Table of Contents

Foreword i

Preface iii

Introduction: Massaging The "Nots" Out Of Your Life 1

Chapter One: Step 1. How to Condition for the Challenge 4

Chapter Two: Mary Tilton's Reflection 23

Chapter Three: Step 2. Become an Effective Communicator 30

Chapter Four: Rob O' Brien's Reflection 47

Chapter Five: Step 3. Dealing with Fear and Anxiety 54

Chapter Six: April Peebles's Reflection 66

Chapter Seven: Step 4. Connecting to People Tools Action 73

Chapter Eight: John Kendrick's Reflection 84

Chapter Nine: Step 5. Enjoy the process 90

Chapter Ten: Catherine Frenes's Reflection 96

Chapter Eleven: Step 6. Running on Fire 103

Chapter Twelve: Adriana Soto's Reflection 108

Chapter Thirteen: Step 7. Celebrating the Victory 112

Chapter Fourteen: Workbook 121

The Authors 160

Introduction

MASSAGING THE "NOTS" OUT OF YOUR LIFE

You are everything that you need. Time is precious and limited. The concept of making the best of your life begins with the strategic and intentional effort of asking these questions: why am I here, and what should I be doing?

On this journey, a few purpose-living friends came together to help you develop a deeper sense of that question and to help you enjoy the benefits of indulging in the answer to finding a purpose for your life.

The metaphor of "massages" will be used at times because they are both enjoyable and healing. One reason is that we need to massage the "nots" out of our comebacks in order to become realigned with our purpose. Living within our purpose is meant to be a healing and enjoyable process.

I began running track at a young age, while attending a private school in Los Angeles, California. While going to this school, I experienced being driven by challenges at an early age, like many others. My mother, being the athlete that she was, joined the parent's track team, setting an example of competition for me.

Finding Purpose

At my very first track meet, I was set at the line, ready to race against my classmates and other students from competing teams. The Starter pointed the starting gun in the air. "On your mark, get set, go!" As the gun fired, I bolted like lightning; at least that was how I felt, only being a couple of feet tall from the ground. I was in first place with my mother shouting, "Go, Stevie, go!

Once I got to the finish line banner, I stopped and looked behind me. Everyone was yelling, "Go! Cross the finish line." Within a couple of seconds, a kid named Sean behind me crossed the line and broke the tape, then I walked across the line, ending up in second place.

What I learned from that experience, was this: In life, we don't need to stop when we get to or close to the finish line. We must cross the finish line, before we look back, because we may lose the race. In high school, I had a tee-shirt that read "second place is the first loser." I felt like I had lost the race, even though I ended up in second place, just because I looked back before crossing the finish line. Sean, the guy who beat me, walked away with a 2-foot trophy with his name and our school name printed on it, and an acknowledgement in a ceremony. I walked away with a ribbon that said, "Second Place."

This experience ate me up inside, but it was a lesson like no other. Not only did I say I will no longer stop at the finish line, but I also vowed that no one would ever beat me again without me giving all that I had. Though I've won many races since then, and lost some, I always kept the drive to win.

In life, our shortcomings and challenges should be used as learning experiences; a chance to reflect on the decisions in which we could have been wiser. Anywhere from, maybe I need to surround myself with more positive people, to maybe I should study more for the next test,

Finding Purpose

or even to maybe I will address an issue with more compassion next time so that peoples' responses will be more receptive.

Here, in this book, we are going to explore relevant ways to deal with the challenges of living within our purpose, and "making a comeback" in life. This is all through conditioning exercises, the importance of making timely press releases, as well as meditation/reflection.

Whatever you are facing today, you will begin to move in a direction, where you will soon celebrate the victory!

You, ultimately, know what's best for yourself, more than anyone else. The world is a loud place. There are an innumerable amount of things screaming at you all day: coworkers, spouses, children, religious communities, neighbors, family, friends, PTA, commercials, movies, politicians. - Mary Tilton

---

Chapter One

STEP 1. HOW TO CONDITION FOR THE CHALLENGE

NOTES

Finding, Managing, Sacrificing Time:
Massaging the "not" out of "I do Not have Time" Conditioning

Purpose is an element of life that is essential to achieving well-being and is best acquired through means of well-thought-out preparation. Before finding purpose, conditioning our mind, spirit, body, and emotional state is crucial. Following this outlook, the activity of conditioning before approaching challenges is absolutely necessary.

BEING READY

This would apply if, for instance, someone were to tell an aspiring recording artist, "You are not getting that record deal because your music isn't good enough." Getting that response could inspire that artist to tell themselves, "I need to build my confidence up because if I

Finding Purpose

keep getting rejected, I need to depend on my confidence to stay positive." But it could also cause someone in a similar position to quit.

When you condition, you have built your confidence before receiving a rejection, just in case it happens to occur. What may seem like a significant rejection could just be a minor challenge that you would need conditioning for? Embracing the benefits of conditioning can make you ready for these types of challenges well before even a sign of their existence. This approach is like being ready before you have to get ready.

The first thing we must do to make a comeback after a setback is to figure out how we are going to use our time to develop ourselves. Being an athlete for most of my life, I can relate to the importance of staying in shape during my off-season. In any sport, a season of practice and games only takes up a portion of the year. This means that if I want to have an edge once the season starts, it is imperative to train in the off-season, months ahead of time. I had to take time out, in order to stand out.

In high school, track season would typically start around January, which was when we would meet as a team and condition our physical bodies to start competing within three weeks' time. During my senior year, the team captains would lead the others in exercise and stretching activities. We would all leave the locker room, and joke around until around 3:45 pm; then, the show was on. I'd give the first stretch then eventually transition to drills until we reached the 400meter lap around the track. The rule was: keep up, don't fall too far behind. At this point, the real practice would start.

My team had intense, strenuous workouts to prepare for those our meets. I knew that holding my position meant I had to be prepared to take on every workout the coach handed down in order to prove my position as a leader on the team. Many people ended up getting sick throughout the first week of the season, which eventually developed into them quitting and giving up. It was not enough for me to just keep up, because I had to stand out.

When should you start conditioning? Do you wait for the challenge to start? Do you wait until you are expected to compete or perform? If so, you are behind the game. Waiting to prepare, then expecting to perform once the challenge begins places you in a position of always trying to catch up.

Identifying my Present Condition

That previous November, after football season, I would go to a gym near home in Marietta, Georgia, and get a body fat composition test to measure the condition of my physical health. Afterwards, we would take a blood pressure test, followed by a conditioning test on the treadmill.

The results of these tests would be recorded on paper since they all involved measurable data. The track team would take these collected measurements, then study them to determine what areas we were lacking in physically, and what would be considered the smartest strategies to work on those areas that needed improvement.

Let's say I had 9% body fat, and my desired percentage was 6%. To achieve this goal, I would normally have to incorporate more cardio in my program and slightly reduce my intake of carbohydrates. If my endurance was low on the treadmill, I would have to run at decent speeds for longer periods of time to increase it. If my strength was weak in my legs, I would need to do more quad exercises. If my flexibility did not have enough elasticity, that could be treated by incorporating more stretching. I had to come up with a plan focusing on certain details more than others and to do that, I had to be able to identify my shortcomings first.

Have you taken the time to assess your composition in life right now? Before you make any serious moves toward building or progressing, you must ask yourself a few questions and take yourself through a few tests. Before living your purpose effectively, it is critical that you figure out your composition, or where your current condition stands mentally, emotionally, physically, and spiritually.

Developing a Personal Approach to Change

There are questions regarding the issue of change you can ask yourself, such as: do I need to change? If so, how should go about it? Would this be a gradual thing, or would I want to put myself through some sort of boot camp-style process, possibly locking myself in a room for two weeks, or going on a weekend retreat? What is it that would work best for you?

Bringing your Mind to a Healthy Condition

Have I taken the time to educate myself enough on the types of challenges that I will be facing in the future?

What recourses can I access in the case that I need psychological direction to deal with the challenge(s) at hand? i.e. books, internet, library resources, classes, experienced advisors, etc.

Deciding to use psychological resources when necessary does not make you unintelligent, but rather, makes you wise. A man was once quoted as saying, "A wise man is not one who memorizes the dictionary, but a wise man is the one who always has access to the dictionary."

Balancing your Emotions to a Healthy Condition

Ask yourself, have I taken the time to build my emotional strength and balance to handle pressure at this moment? If not, identify some issues you may be dealing with, such as harbored feelings you may be holding deep inside; the feelings of hurt from that person who told you "I never want to see your face again;" or, the family member who borrowed money from you two years ago and never paid it back. Figure out within you, is this thing worth holding on to? Can this situation be reconciled, or addressed, or should I simply let it go? If you do choose to let your issue go, here are some examples of some techniques that may help you:

Write the situation down in full detail of what someone has done to you as if you're speaking to them.

Example: Last year you cheated on me.

Example: You borrowed money and never paid it back.

Write down what you feel their intentions were for taking the action they took.

Example: I feel you did this just to hurt me because I was nothing but faithful and giving to you.

Write down, exactly how you feel about what they did to you.

Example: I am hurt, and it brings me to tears when I think about it.

Write down what they should or should not have done to you versus what they did.

Example: If you were not happy with me, you could have either told me where we could have improved our relationship, or you could have let me go. I would have handled that better.

Write down why you have to let this situation go.

Example: I have to let go of the situation because it has been holding me back from moving on into something healthy.

Write down the message, "I am letting this situation go as of now."

Example: If you feel that the situation is not repairable, you may want to burn the paper, which would symbolize burning the hurt that you are holding on to. That said, if you think that the situation is reparable, you have a decision to make: you can either send it or burn it. In many cases, you would still want to burn that paper.

While the paper burns, you must pray to God or your higher power to be strengthened from resolving that situation. Pray that you will learn something from that situation, and pray for peace from it. In other words, you have let it go! Once this process has been accomplished, the process of healing can be considered to be truly underway.

In some instances, it may require professional counseling to be healed from instances of hurt, whether it comes from a spiritual leader or a traditional therapist. You may want to also include holistic care, such as cardio exercises, yoga, eating a healthy diet, and things of that nature. Healing from emotional hurt does not have a cookie-cutter approach, and may require a combination of the elements listed above, along with other techniques that have thus far been unnamed.

Bringing your Physical Being to a Healthy Condition

Are you taking the proper time out to care for your physical being? One thing I suggest to do every year is to get a physical exam. Our physical condition is very important to how we function mentally throughout the day as we fulfill our purpose.

Finding Purpose

Imagine a person who lives 60 miles away from their job, and considers the two hours of sitting in traffic they have to do as they travel to and from work every day. On the other hand, compare that to a coworker of theirs who may live in a loft about 5 miles from the office, and thus would have a much shorter commute to the same job. Based on this alone, and without any other factors, the latter's stress levels at the end of each day may very likely be significantly lower.

In this scenario, you have two different people with the same job, but one who goes through more job-related stress than the other due to their commute alone. As we all know, your stress levels directly affects your blood pressure. As your blood pressure rises, it is reducing the amount of blood flowing to the brain, which then reduces brain functionality. This is a prime example of how our physical condition affects our thinking.

Being tested and getting correct cholesterol levels, glucose levels, and other relevant readings will tell us the measures we need to take, to increase our brain activity, sharpen our thinking, and increase our mind's ability to handle situations we may meet with. This is the type of testing that helps keep us from "breaking" or becoming "mentally overwhelmed", which is important because we must know where our physical body stands in regard to health and condition of well-being.

It is recommended that you get three days of exercise per week, whether it's walking, running, or some other form of cardio, for 45 minutes each day. One should include 15 or 20 minutes of weight resistance training in each workout, with the approval of a physician. As a result, you will likely feel much better, and your mind will probably function much sharper. This seemingly small thing can make a huge difference, as well as eating healthier, low cholesterol food that is also lower in saturated fats, salts, and sugars. It can get tough sometimes, but actions turn into habits, and we're doing this together.

Connecting to my Disposition/Spiritual Conditioning

Are you taking time to reflect on what your moral anchor is? It is important not to give up when push comes to shove, and when efforts need to be made because this is when decisions can be detrimental to you, your friends, and your family.

I've known many types of people in my life who would be considered successful, who have faced the regrets of taking shortcuts to get where they wanted to be, from the straightedge kid who is now addicted to drugs, to the CEO reporting false information to the IRS. Sometimes these types of behaviors come with levels of entitlements during certain points of life, as they receive a monetary gain for work they have not fully achieved. Other times these behaviors are conducted through desperation. It is beneficial to know before you get involved with something if your feeling on the issue is "this will be my disposition if things don't go my way."

It has been said that "rejection is God's protection," so if you've worked hard to receive something, maybe you're not getting the rewards you expect simply because you should be moving in a different direction, or maybe your time for your goal to become materialized may not have arrived yet. This is like saying to yourself, "I am standing on a disposition of not making irresponsible moves when I get impatient."

Finding Purpose

We all get impatient at times but having to wait is a part of growing and appreciating what we receive after working hard, and waiting for that "thing." A useful solution to rely on when we are getting impatient is to keep working hard and rest assured that we will soon be rewarded for our diligence, hard work, and patience. It is important to acknowledge that when we work hard, we are building knowledge, wisdom and character within us in whatever we are doing. This can apply even when working on the job we don't care for, as I've mentioned in a previous book.

Maybe our boss isn't recognizing or promoting us to the marketing position we feel we deserve to receive. When we are in that position, there is always much to learn and take with us, even if we were to end up leaving the company. Some people in this position may start committing such infractions as stealing supplies out of the boss's office or trying to tap into the payroll's computer and manipulate the system.

What a person who would follow that course of behavior may not realize is that now they are setting themselves up to get caught for a crime that they would get fired and arrested for, which would prevent them from utilizing their work experience for any other company in the future.

Your position does not make you. Your money does not make you. You make you. You are made by the integrity in your decisions and the value of the virtues that you see in yourself. This is one reason that I express to people how the value of your bank account is now what gives you value as a person, but simply exists as a value in your account. Mastering yourself, in the sense of identifying your positive character and living by it, as well as identifying your negative characteristics and disposing of them, is what makes you valuable. In this sense, it is

Finding Purpose

beneficial to connect to the position you will take when things get difficult and connect to your disposition.

TIME

Part A

Taking the "not" out of I Do Not Have Time

When making a decision to find or live in your purpose, we must take an extensive look at our time, namely how we manage it, save it, and sacrifice for it. Many people that I have spoken with regarding the topic of purpose have informed me that they live in default because they do not have time to design their life. If we are not being strategic with our time, it is impossible to live a life within our purpose.

It is recommended that we do Time Management Evaluations often. Here we will discuss ways to manage our time through activities like condensing responsibilities into consolidated slots and eliminating procrastination.

Overbooking

Many times our problem with time management is simply overcommitting ourselves, especially to meet the needs of others. This would apply if someone invited you to a meeting so you could collaborate on a new business idea that you may not feel you are quite ready to discuss, or if someone were to give you an unrealistic deadline to finish an important report. Usually, when speaking of those who overbook themselves for obligations, they are the same people who come across as "flakey". They often cancel on plans, or just don't show up at all. They end up with the image they were trying to avoid, which is the stigma of not being dependable. To combat this type of development, you should be realistic when someone asks you for your services. If someone needs your services, it should be expected that they will be flexible, and if they are not, things could end up spinning out of your control. Ask yourself, how could this possibly serve my life's purpose?

Depending Too Much on Us

Another problem with time management is the faux pas of simply not writing things down. Relying only on our minds to keep track of things will fail us and fail us often. Such is the case when you schedule that doctor's appointment for your niece and forget about it until you're reminded about it the day it is supposed to happen, once you realize you have already double-booked that time frame with other obligations. Then we hear a familiar expression such as "there just isn't enough time in a day."

This normally creates tension for us, and causes anxiety, from simply not writing what we would consider a small task down on paper. This type of situation becomes a substantial problem when it gets in the way of the agenda that we intended to remember. Of course, there are times we must depend on our memory when not having the opportunity to write things down on paper, or on a device such as a smartphone, but still, it is a good idea to write information down when we can.

Procrastination Today, Puts our Purpose on Hold

Remember that business idea you had? Or the new product you once had ambitions to design? Many of us have had so many great ideas, yet never took the time out to develop them, due to saying "I'll get to that someday."

Let me stop you here; you do have time. It's about priorities. Imagine if you sacrificed watching your favorite television show for one year, and took that hour slot that you use each week, or each day for some, and dedicated that time to developing the idea you once felt would demand too much out of your obligation time. Remember, thanks to technology, you can stream those TV shows later in the week, or rent the entire season and watch it at a more convenient time.

I heard a funny quote once that said, "Why do it today when I can put it off until tomorrow." In contrast, I subscribe to the notion that if we do it today, we can enjoy the benefits of the results tomorrow. This approach can also help because it can help you clear your mind and re-gear your focus on something more future productive. When we procrastinate, it's like we trap our minds, keeping them stuck by focusing on the things of the past until we complete them.

I don't know if you have ever done this as a kid, but there were times in my childhood when I remember playing outside with my neighborhood friends, and when I had a sudden urge to use the restroom, I would do my best to hold it as long as possible so that it wouldn't interfere with my fun time. I didn't care that I could get a bladder infection, or even worse. I didn't even care so much about the discomfort I was feeling from not going to the restroom when I should have. I would dance around until I felt like I was going to explode, and then run home full speed to use the restroom. I would even try blocking my need to relieve myself out of my mind, but ultimately it would not work because of my body's discomfort.

Similarly, some of us need to release that report we are thinking about and stop dancing around it, trying to ease the discomfort of not doing it. Once we release that thing that is procrastinating over, we will just feel better. So my advice is, don't be like me as a kid. Sometimes obligations will get in the way of our "playtime", but tackling our task at hand makes us feel so much more relaxed at the end of the day. By the way, wouldn't you like to enjoy that income your efforts can generate now, instead of putting it off and possibly never gaining the benefits?

Organizing the Time

When it comes to keeping track of time effectively, I would recommend using an old-fashioned, pocket-sized monthly calendar, done in what is commonly also known as the "At A Glance" style. When you book the great details of your schedule on your smartphone, or in your organizer, at least jot a brief note in the pocket calendar with the time, personal details, and task. It's just a quick reference that is easily accessible, but it can truly make a world of difference.

Tell someone you live with, or a person you interact with often, such as a significant other, or close friend, about the appointment that you have. Ask them to remind you if it comes to their mind. I use this technique for things that are extremely important to me. I will write it down, but I will also turn to someone I spend a lot of time around and say, "I have this really important day on next Saturday. If it comes to your mind anytime between here and there, could you remind me?" There's nothing wrong with being safe, and taking out as many precautions as you can.

How many alarm clocks do you wake up to in the morning? I hope at least two. Set two alarms when there is an appointment you need to attend at a certain time. This can be helpful in many relevant situations, such as the electricity going out at night, or you forgetting to charge your cell phone the night before your important meeting. When working job shifts as early as 4 am, I have awakened in the middle of the night and turned alarms off without even realizing what I

Finding Purpose

was doing. I call it "waking up drunk," meaning when you wake up and turn an alarm off, not knowing exactly what you are doing, before you pass out again.

My grandmother used to say to me every morning while I would head out to school, "Embrace this moment right now, we will never have it again." Though we get other moments, each one we live on is precious. The moments we spend with our family and our friends are times that we will never get to experience again, and we pray that we will get more moments with our loved ones each day. As we accomplish our every day goals and tasks, it is also a great habit to embrace them as we achieve and receive them.

TIME

Part B

Making Time - Let's briefly discuss
how we can create the time that we currently do not have.

In the case that you have organized your time, but still feel there isn't enough to meet all of your obligations, it may be time to do an evaluation. This is a good time to figure out what the most important things are that need to be done, and how to keep them on schedule. The smaller items or obligations may have to be postponed, but definitely not through procrastinating.

When you procrastinate, you have the ability to do something now, but you are choosing to do it later. When you postpone something, you are deciding that you do not have the efficient time to do it right now so you reschedule it to a more appropriate time, or cancel the obligation altogether. There will be times when your human self, as anyone's human self, thinks that something can get done in a certain time frame but, as time unfolds, you have to concede to yourself, "Sorry, but I can't make it happen." Allow yourself to be human, admit and release the mistake when bookings become too consuming and large.

Have Someone Scratch Your Back

Most times, there are people around you who will, as the saying goes, "Scratch your back." Sometimes we as humans will think in the box and forget the people who may exist outside of that proverbial zone. I will ask for a favor without a problem, especially after I've done favors for others.

Let's say you have to pick up a prescription in the South Bay and you have a meeting around the same time that is taking place on the west side. It would be quite beneficial to realize "Oh, I have a friend in the South

Bay who is unemployed," and decide to ask for help from your friend in the area. You could ask, "Hey Amber, could you do me a favor and I'll even give you gas money. I have to pick up a prescription before 9 pm when the pharmacy closes, and I'll be in a meeting until 9 pm. Could you pick it up, and I'll get it from your house around 10 pm." A friend in her position would usually say something like, "Yeah sure, and you don't have to pay me for it." By choosing this approach to getting your activities done, you've just made a great time and satisfied all of your obligations.

Packaging Time

It is highly advisable to consolidate obligations whenever you can. If I'm due for my yearly medical exam, for example, as well as my dental teeth cleaning, I will do my best to book them to occur on the same day. If I have 10 life coach meetings with clients for the week, I will do my best to split those appointments between two days, and have many of them in the same location. That way, when they can come to me, it saves me time from having to drive around the entire city, which can do wonders for my performance via the benefits that can come from effective time management.

I will also consolidate having dinner with a friend and business associate and have that same outing serve as a business meeting. That way, we can speak on ideas, and possibly get some work done.

Finding Purpose

Following that train of thought, we would be able to have a two hour meal, and complete two hours' worth of work, all at the same time.

In another instance, if it's time to go away to visit family on the other coast of the U.S., you take some of your work with you and set certain times in the day that you will obligate towards work, such as in the evening before you go to bed. By doing this, even a time slot as quick as 15 or 20 minutes can make a powerful difference. Plus, you'd be surprised what a new environment can do to your work's creativity.

Sacrifice for Time

Sometimes we just need to sacrifice, in order to make time. There is a balance in accomplishing this, and balance is important. There will be moments in life where we have to ask ourselves, "how important is this thing I want or need to do?" We have 24 hours in a day, and the average person spends around 8 – 9 of them at work. That means we have about 15 to 16 hours left that we can divide into personal leisure and sleep. Maybe we have to cut into our sleep for a week in order to get that project done, or not hang out with our best friend for a month, but it is important to decide which aspect of your lifestyle to forgo temporarily in order to get things done.

Sacrifice is never easy, or it would not be truly considered a sacrifice. Sacrifice means to give up something important, for a return of something even greater. When we focus on the greater return, it helps us release the value from the thing that we are sacrificing. Sacrifice is a measure of faith. We must be willing to sacrifice our leisure time, and sometimes even a couple of hours of sleep, in order to receive that big return in our lives.

When I was boxing, I hired a personal trainer, because I knew he would push me and stay on my case when I did not want to show up

Finding Purpose

for training. I didn't miss one day, either. I knew that if I missed a day of training, he would train me even harder when I returned because he wanted to keep me on track. This is partly because my success is representative of him.

What's funny is that before I started working with him, I convinced myself that I didn't have enough time to commit to boxing. The reality was, I did, and that I just needed an extra push to do so at the time. The workouts were very intense. There was a clock on the upper wall that had a green, yellow, and red light. Throughout the training, the light would turn green while we trained hard for about 3 minutes, then it would turn yellow for about ten seconds, then it would turn red and stay red for about 60 seconds, and then it would turn green as we began training again.

Following this timing system, my trainer and I didn't have time to talk and play around, so we would focus on resting in the downtime because we knew the light would turn green again. It was fun, but training as a boxer is tough, as many of you know. The reason boxers are able to achieve so much in such a short amount of time, such as losing 20 pounds in 2 weeks, is that they compact their activities and drill themselves intensively even through their tiredness. They have to be wise like us, and not work themselves to their death, but push themselves to a healthy physical limit, to accomplish their goals in a designated amount of time. They sacrifice and focus on boxing in the brisk time frames that they are allotted, and it isn't easy.

I've been to boxing gyms where the fighters lived at the gym as they trained for their next fight. They would live, eat, and sleep boxing until they accomplished their training goal. By doing this, they would receive all of the benefits that would come with their sacrifice.

Finding Purpose

I recommend that you reward yourself while doing this so you won't burn out. When I was boxing at Freddie Roache's gym, I would go to some of the local boxing matches and enjoy the competition as a reward to myself for training so tough. If you're writing a book, maybe you can go to a place on the weekend that clears your mind, like viewing the cliff in Palos Verde's, CA, which overlooks the edge of great green grass over the clouds as you can look down in the blue ocean waters from hundreds of feet up. Rewarding yourself in these personally satisfying types of ways can make your process much more pleasing.

Let's not linger on the big setback, but ponder on the big comeback. Let's make time to find and live in our purpose, and condition ourselves for greater success. It will be worth it.

Tools to organize your time:
Pocket Calendar, Outlook, Cell phone, wall calendar, to-do list.

Chapter Two

MARY TILTON'S REFLECTION

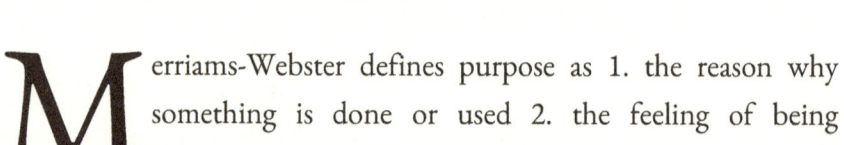

Merriams-Webster defines purpose as 1. the reason why something is done or used 2. the feeling of being determined to do or achieve something 3. the aim or goal of a person: what a person is trying to do, become, etc.

If you are a semi-self-aware person, chances are you have wondered why you are here? Maybe you have even gone beyond that and pondered why you are here – in this place –at this time? While the definition laid out by Webster and Merriam certainly involves the notion of ACTION, I'm going to take you to another point of view. It's one I can share with you only because it's one I have gained through my own experiences. My hope is that it will give you a deeper understanding of PURPOSE and help you on your way to finding yours.

The aspect of purpose I want to talk about is being who you truly are. You are YOU for a reason, for a purpose. As Dr. Seuss says in his book <u>Happy Birthday to You!</u>, "Today you are you, that is truer than true. There is no one alive who is you-er than you." Let that sink in. Not just on your birthday, but every day of your life you are a unique

Finding Purpose

individual. There is NO ONE LIKE YOU in all of the population of the earth, which as I write this is at 7.4 billion. That's pretty amazing.

Now that you have that image in your mind, we move on to the next step, and this is the meat of what I'm going to share. Who are you, you mighty individual? It is imperative that you find out who you really are – inside and out. The good, the bad, the ugly. You're going to have to do some digging if you want to discover your foundation. Now, before you start belly-aching and saying things like: "But Mary, that's too much work" or "There are some things in there I don't want to let out," let me explain something to you.

Unless you are willing to accept who you are in all of your glory AND dishonor, you will not reach your highest potential. You will not even be able to fully live. It's not enough to admit these things. You have to find a way to accept and love these aspects of you, ALL of them.

M. Scott Peck wrote one of my favorite books of all time called <u>The Road Less Traveled: A New Psychology of Love, Traditional Values, and Spiritual Growth</u>. Seriously, read this book. In it, he says, "Human beings are poor examiners, subject to superstition, bias, prejudice, and a PROFOUND tendency to see what they want to see rather than what is really there." And also, "Problems do not go away. They must be worked through or else they remain, forever a barrier to the growth and development of the spirit."

I think one of the reasons this book appeals to me so much is that I have to stay active in being honest with myself. It's not something I've achieved necessarily (my rose-colored glasses blur my vision from time to time) but rather something I try to make continual progress in. Raw honesty is a must if you wish to move forward in your purpose.

Finding Purpose

Since I've established the essentialness of self-discovery, let's talk for a second about how to do that. I have done A LOT of work on myself. I have read books, I have kept journals, I have prayed, I have meditated, I have been in therapy (for several years). I have learned my strengths and weaknesses. I have sought out the dark corners of my mind, faced things I didn't want to face, admitted things I didn't want to admit. Carrying around the weight of the life experiences I've had was debilitating and confusing, and what was worse, I wasn't even aware of it.

Carl Jung says, "Until we make the unconscious conscious, it will direct your life and you will call it fate." For example, how many failed relationships have you had that you blamed on the other person without taking responsibility for your part? Even if your partner was an untrustworthy and unreliable person, this theory says your part could be as simple as attracting someone like that in the first place.

You may not have deliberately sought an unscrupulous person, but you ended up in that situation. The best thing you can do is ask yourself "why?" Another example may be a job you are unhappy with. You have the ability to get your resume together, job-hunt, talk to a head-hunter or speak to your boss about how your strengths could be utilized more effectively, but if you remain in it and just complain that the universe is conspiring to prevent you from having a job you like, it's your own fault.

If you are willing to observe the side of yourself that is making decisions for you, there will be a level of healing you've never known before. It's one of the hardest and most terrifying things I've ever done, but if you don't shrink back from it, a new life awaits you.

Finding Purpose

This is also the time I'd like to mention that it is imperative for you to be brave and diligent but also to be gentle with yourself. You, ultimately, know what's best for yourself, more than anyone else. The world is a loud place. There are an innumerable amount of things screaming at you all day: coworkers, spouses, children, religious communities, neighbors, family, friends, PTA, commercials, movies, politicians. All telling you what you should do, where you should be, what you should look like, how you should act, what to believe. Whether from a place of love or a know-it-all attitude, these many voices do not fully know what's right for you. You may ask, how do I turn them off? but you can't. They will always be competing for your attention and expect your obedience, so you have to practice tuning them out.

Take some time. Be alone. Be still. Be Quiet. Listen. This is where you may realize that what you have been striving for doesn't require striving at all. It only means settling into what you already are. Through the cobwebs and dust and recesses of your mind, behind the boxes and broken lamps and tossed aside moments of your life, there is YOU. Magnificent you. Waiting ever so patiently for the day you come looking to discover yourself.

"Self-improvement can have temporary results, but lasting transformation occurs only when we honor ourselves as the source of wisdom and compassion." - Pema Chodron, <u>The Places That Scare You: A Guide to Fearlessness in Difficult Times.</u>

In addition to being gentle, a sense of humor and curiosity will serve you well. For instance, I am insanely curious. I'm not quite sure if it's a good thing or a bad thing that I know a little about a lot of things and have probably forgotten more than I remember, but I'm going

Finding Purpose

with it. I'm enjoying myself. I learn and take in information from almost anywhere.

Speaking of Dr. Seuss, I re-read <u>Oh, the Places You'll Go!</u> regularly. I get so much from that and many other children's books when my son and I read them together. I look at art. I enjoy nature. I "meet" new people on Facebook and follow random groups. I take inspiration anywhere I get it. I can find a life lesson at the grocery store next to the milk. It's just how I choose to live.

There's a very intelligent man I follow on Facebook. A lot of things he posts are above my head. I'm not going to lie, he makes my brain hurt. But one thing he shared really resonated with me. I keep a screenshot of it on my phone. I don't want to lose it because I hope I always look at problems this way:

"You want to approach every problem, fear, concern, or challenge with a little piece of the guy who cracks bank vaults, or a cat burglar who is an expert at high-stakes capers. There is more treasure inside the structure of any problem than can be found in any vault on earth; but to make use of it, you have to learn the tricks of the trade. How to approach the thing correctly, how to learn its structure, defuse 'the alarms', confuse the sentries, bust the circuits, crack the security measures, and shake the door. Once inside? Paradise. Inside every problem is a library of solutions worth more than any vault can hold. It's all in the approach, the attention, the skill, the technique...and the insistent compulsion to reach not only into excellence...but beyond..."
- Darin Stevenson

Now after all this talk about YOU, I want to say that even though it is personal to you, your purpose pervades your family, your community, your city, your country, your world. It's going to involve

Finding Purpose

the welfare of the earth and its inhabitants. Whether it is evident to you or not, realizing and acting on your purpose shifts the landscape of things. It gives meaning to your life and meaning to the lives of those around you.

I used to think my purpose would be lived out in the career I chose, motherhood and family, religion and how I served and worshipped, or the organizations I volunteer in. I only knew I wanted to make a difference (with a vision of me flying through the air, cape fluttering in the wind). The truth is, it is found in all of those things because my purpose is first lived out in who I already am, who I've always been. What I demonstrate on a daily basis, what I put out in the world in my life, is just as important as any widespread project I choose to be a part of.

How I handle myself at work affects multiple people in one day. How I love and parent my child affects him and anyone he comes into contact with that day. Then, those "small" moments echo down the line. My clients will run errands and interact with others or go home to their families, and who knows if something I said or did will influence their connections to others? My son will grow into a man and have a family of his own, and during this time as he grows, I am guiding his future decisions. Don't cut yourself short by thinking your purpose in life is only validated if it's seen by a lot of people. The smallest of actions or inactions is reverberating further than you know.

You have a reason for being here. You are important. If you want to find and understand what that may be, you must first believe that one actually exists for you. Then, start digging. Once you do all this soul-excavating, perhaps even while you're doing it, your purpose will make itself known to you. You'll find where your gifts are, and you'll learn what side of yourself you need to keep in check in order to be effective in exhibiting those gifts. I leave you with lots of love and just a few more quotes.

"How little do we know that which we are! How less what we may be!" - Lord Byron "Don Juan"

"The most successful people are those who don't have any illusion about who they are. They know themselves well and they can move in the direction of their best talents. They know the kind of culture they thrive in and how they can benefit from that culture. Unfortunately, most people don't understand themselves. Most people don't want to lose their illusions about themselves, although they say they want to take charge of their career." - Bud Bray, quoted in "Is it too Late to Run Away and Join the Circus?"

"Knowing yourself is the beginning of all wisdom." - Aristotle

After about ten years of personal training, I realized that one could only get someone to their physical goals so far. I was essentially a therapist to my clients, talking about their aspirations and their fears and what was keeping them from reaching their goals and the life they wanted in the current moment. - Rob O'Brien

Chapter Three

STEP 2. BECOME AN EFFECTIVE COMMUNICATOR

NOTES

Become an Effective Communicator:
Massaging the "not" out of – I am Not an Effective Communicator

This chapter is about interacting with people. In order to find purpose, it is important that we communicate effectively. We must be able to effectively explain what we want and need, as well as hear the wants and needs of others. This could be a strength or a weakness during certain times in your past, but it is essential that you continue to grow in this area, from this day moving forward. It should be very apparent in your current and ongoing communication is healthy, regardless of your past experiences.

Elevator Pitch

Finding Purpose

So many American musical artists have retired in the past years and decided to make a comeback with a new product. such as a music video or an album. They will make their announcement to a selected audience, primarily made up of their fans, and announce, "I'm making a comeback." This comeback could be one or two years in the making, such as with R&B singer "Maxwell", and the goal would be for his fans to anticipate his return for many reasons.

One way that an artist could set off such a comeback is to acknowledge themselves, and their dynamic talents and abilities. The artist could engage in an inner dialogue, saying, "I'm going to do this because I know it is in me to do it." That is what Michael Jackson said to himself for his last "This Is It" tour. "I'm doing this one last time because it is still in me".

Another reason an artist will make this type of announcement is the obligation he will feel after making it to actually get it done. Also, that artist could be motivated by feeling the support of his **cheerleaders** as an encouragement to fight through the discouraging times he may face during his training. There is a reason why Maxwell and other celebrities do not set up press conferences with the paparazzo to make that announcement, and that is because people consider the paparazzi to be discouragers. The discouragers will find out about the comeback, and many times attempt to interrupt it, so in that respect, it helps someone in an artist's position not to pay them any attention.

If you notice on shows that consist of content sourced from the paparazzi, or the magazines that their material is published in, they typically prey on the shortcomings of the people that they are speaking of. It is a reasonable observation that they do it for a buck, and that buck likely makes them feel good or at least makes them feel satisfied that they have been rewarded for identifying a flaw in a celebrity that no one else knew existed.

When you think about it, most of us have "paparazzi" in our lives, all around us. Sometimes we call them friends, and other times we call them family. This is why it is crucial to identify the people in your life who will cheer you on, and the ones who will discourage you, and share your comeback with the constructive people who share your everyday experience.

Some people say that you shouldn't announce it to anyone, and just come back. Well, that kind of approach is probably ideal for a perfect world, but we live in a human world. And in our world, we typically enjoy sharing big moves we are making with someone who can function as an encourager while we make that move. The important factor in doing so is to share it with the right people and to share it in the appropriate way. In this way, you are your own Public Representative.

The Public Representative

The task of hiring the best Public Representative you can find means finding someone who is passionate about the topic and the person that they are representing. Many people consider their Public Reps to be their friends. I must say, there has to be a high level of trust for a person to take on this position, because you will end up telling them things the general public does not know, and it is their job to filter out what should be shared with the populous, and what should be kept private.

The trust you would have in your PR Rep is crucial to pulling off a successful comeback. Now I'm not specifically referring to when you legitimately need to make the professional public announcement to

Finding Purpose

always represent yourself, but my point is this: when you are representing yourself and announcing to family, friends, and associates that you are making some type of significant comeback, your should be wise about what you share, and who you share it with.

It's crazy how the things we say can "make us or break us", but many people who have made the mistake will attest to it being true. Sometimes when a person is upset with someone else, it's a similar effect to the media being in your face, taking verbal shots at you, and waiting for a negative reaction. That reaction is usually emotionally driven and used against us in a confrontational manner. They will use that reaction to judge your character and explain how it is offensive. This kind of carrying-on can hurt our movement towards living out our purpose by interrupting relationships that we would otherwise depend on to help fulfill our purpose. The ultimate result would not be a good representation for ourselves.

When we are fulfilling the role of a good Public Rep for ourselves, it's a good decision to start speaking positively in the public's eye, focus on the strengths that exist within you, and speak favorably to our supporters. There may be times when the discouragers would need to be addressed but, for the most part, good Public Reps don't address them too often. In fact, it is a good chance that the discouragers probably won't change, especially since they can stand to make a buck off of their exploitation of your flaws.

I would address people publicly by telling them: "I've been gone for a long time, faced some setbacks, but in this time I've been able to regain focus and perfect myself. I've been training and I've seen that I still have it. As I make my comeback I want to thank all of the encouraging people who have supported me, and I thank you in advance for your continued support."

Or, you could say something like: "I have discovered the abilities I have in my conditioning process, and this was partly the reason for making this decision. The other part was just my will and desire, and the love for what I do."

As you probably noticed, in my hypothetical comment, I didn't give a comeback date. I just said I was coming back and suggested that it may even be soon. Once a particular time is established, it's your choice to announce it, but it is mandatory that you stick to it. As you tell your supporters you are making the move, and thank them for supporting you, they will likely feel empowered. They feel a sense of accomplishment for helping you, and this is great because we need the help of people to fulfill our purpose.

We need cheerleaders. When fulfilling our purpose, there will be challenges you've never seen before. Circumstances will surface that will make us or break us. It will either build our character or compromise it. How we respond to our times of struggle and challenge is everything.

Sometimes we may not realize the level of strength that is within us. There will be moments when we need to borrow that strength from others, whether through encouraging words, wisdom from someone we trust, or financial assistance. It isn't good to live like you're on an island, or isolated from close interaction with the rest of the world. Our cheerleaders will root for us in our weakest moments and should root for us in our strongest, in order for us to finish strong. We may not always see eye to eye with everyone who supports us, but we will always know that they are on our team and that their intentions are always in our best interest. Simply put, cheerleaders want us to win.

Communication - # 1 Factor in Relationships

I want to take some time out to speak on the topic of communication. Being an effective communicator goes far beyond the initial "I'm Coming Back" announcement, but it must be practiced throughout the journey to your purpose. This is similar to the scenario of a man walking up to a young lady and introducing himself, saying "Hello, my name is Shady. I couldn't help but notice how beautiful your earrings are."

What's interesting about this approach is that it involves him not complimenting her like most other guys would be expected to. Instead, it entails him bringing up something that most guys wouldn't normally notice, which in this case is her earrings. She'd probably even have forgotten the fact that his name was "Shady", which would not necessarily be a reference to a cool place out of the sun.

One thing to learn at an early age is that when you have effective communication, you have a better way of getting what you want. That said, the problem that most guys tend to face is this: as effective as their communication is in their initial contact with their significant others, their communication throughout the relationship is usually not nearly as effective. This is typically the time when the lady tends to gravitate towards focusing on their communication as a couple. I hear many guys often saying, "All she wants to do is talk." I'm sure many women who hear this end up thinking, "If I wouldn't have let you talk when you asked me out, we wouldn't be together."

Finding Purpose

Now I'm not perfect, but like some guys reading this book, I get it. The communication between two partners has to be placed at a high priority in order for them to enjoy the benefits of their union. We are all different as people, and we interpret most things based on our personal beliefs and experiences. This means that sometimes we have to explain the intentions of our actions to others.

The Active Listener

How frustrating would the following scenario be?

Let's say a host was conducting a television show, and when was time for questions someone stood up and asked, "I get headaches when I eat too many salty, fried foods, why is that?" The host Dr. would answer "Eating fried salty foods raises your blood pressure, possibly causing the headaches. Thanks for the question." What if someone else stood up and, in all seriousness, asked, "Dr., I get headaches when I eat fried foods and add lots of salt, why is that?" The host would realize that the second person had asked exactly the same question, and probably think, "Are you serious?"

I've heard ladies tell me in the past, "why are you asking that question when I just answered it?" I would say "Oh, can you tell me again, I didn't hear you." Frustrated, she would say "No, you heard me, but you weren't listening."

Sometimes guys just need what is said to be reiterated so that we can get a better understanding. Although many times we do hear what's being said to us, we fail to internalize it, which is the true definition of listening. The task of understanding what's being told to us as it is being said is what could be considered effective communication. This is an ongoing effort in being a good listener, and it is a crucial part of being a good communicator, which again is the foundation of every relationship, both personal and business.

The Retaliator

Positive effective communicators know how to listen to the party speaking to them and receive what they have to say first. The retaliator is just picking apart what's being said to them, as if it's part of a personal attack, and develops a response of retaliation in words before the other person is even finished expressing themselves. This is the catalyst for such incendiary phrases as "Have you been there as I have?" or "Why don't you understand where I'm coming from?"

I recall one particular time when I was being spoken to by a girlfriend who said, "Just let me talk," I responded with, "OK, go ahead." While she was talking, I'm sure she could see it in my eyes that I was thinking, "Yeah, go ahead and finish. I have something to say about that, and that." I wasn't really listening.

Imagine a press conference with the President being asked tough, passionate questions about tax increases. Someone asks, "Mr. President? You promised you would not raise taxes, but you did; now I may lose my home because you broke a promise." What if the President get a boiling mad look on his face as the news reporter was speaking and responded with, "Who are you to tell me I break promises? You don't know half the promises I've kept."

If he did that, it would be apparent that he didn't listen and properly address the issue. The real issue in the case would be the person losing their home. What do you think the appropriate response would have been? Maybe, "I'm sorry you're losing your home, but I had to change my policy." Then maybe he could have offered some direction to help with her issue. That's what I call listening: having understanding, compassion, and empathy for the concerns of what someone else is saying. It makes conversation much more effective when two people are speaking with one another and practicing this technique.

You may be thinking, "If I truly am offended by what someone is saying to me, am I not supposed to respond to it?" In some cases, you should respond to the offensiveness of the statement, but I would suggest always working on responding in a solution-oriented way. Conversation serves no purpose when there is only conflict and no solution. In fact, it just adds fire to the furnace. This is usually the appropriate time to just walk away, and not entertain the offensive statement someone might have directed towards us.

Being a great listener will serve you with great purpose in business and your personal life, causing you to stand out from the common person. While someone is speaking with you, ask yourself the following questions:

What are they saying literally? You should aspire to quote their exact words.
What are they trying to say? This means, what is your interpretation of what they are communicating?
How are they trying to make you feel? Meaning, are the intentions of what they are saying good or bad.
How are they making you feel?
And finally, are they seeking feedback?
After they have completed what they have to say, ask yourself:
What would be a solution-oriented answer?
I would respond with the following approaches:
"This is what you said..." – repeat their exact words.

"Is this what you meant..." – interpret the information and speak it to them

"It sounds like you want me to feel..." – speak on how it seems they want you to feel

"You made me feel like..." – tell them how it truly made you feel

"Ask, did you want my opinion?"

And lastly, tell them a constructive, well-thought-out response.

The Assertive Communicator - Gets Their Way

There was a time when I interviewed for a job at a well-known company, and the process was strenuous. Fortunately, while speaking to the Human Resource worker, I felt a sense of comfort and connection with her. We had a half-hour interview over the phone, and our conversation was followed by an exam. After passing the exam, I had to wait for a phone call for someone to determine whether or not I would land another interview, but this time with the Hiring Manager.

Within a couple of days, I received the call. "Can I have you come in for an interview with the Hiring Manager this Wednesday at 2 pm?" I was at the interview by 12 pm and waited outside the office until about 1:30 pm. Once the Department Manager came into the room to have me meet the Hiring Manager, she walked me to this large conference table, as I was greeted by a lady in a suit who she said loudly, "Hello how are you? Can you have a seat over there, please?" as she pointed to the left side of the table, while she sat at the base. As she pulled out her book of questions, I was thinking to myself, what is this about? She was very respectful and highly professional, but not very comforting. Every question was very direct, as she would repeat, "Please give a specific example." The conversation went like this:

Finding Purpose

Hiring Manager: "I'm going to ask you a series of questions; I need you to give me specific examples as you answer the question with your experiences. The first question is this: 'Had there ever been a time you were asked to carry out a task at work, you felt uncomfortable with while performing the job?'"

Me: "Well I'm sure there where if you're referring to something I may not have had much experience doing."

H: "I need specific examples if you can think of something."

M: "Well, uh, let me see. I know there must have been a time, but I know what I would do if I were in that situation, but I'll try thinking of something in particular".

H: "Ok, good, remember something very specific you've experienced."

The Hiring Manager, as you can tell, was very direct and assertive. She told me what she wanted, and she seemed very sincere when she smiled as she questioned me. She had a great personality, but it was clear that her disposition might not be good for every situation.

Being assertive is basically in its greatest use when you want to appear friendly and respectful, but you want something, or a response, to go in your favor. Still, one must be careful when speaking assertively, because if someone you're speaking to is having a bad day or a difficult time for whatever reason, they may interpret it as being aggressive, or insincere.

So, take precautions if you're trying to achieve effective communication. It can work to your advantage to be assertive if you're conscious of who you're speaking to, and their mood at the moment. It can be very convincing to people, causing many to even second-guess themselves. That said, an assertive speaker who is truly effective speaks with much confidence, not arrogance.

The Aggressive Communicator - Respected by Many, Loved by Few

"Hey you, come here for a second." Have you ever worked with a guy who spoke to you in this way? We're talking about the aggressive communicator. While working in the entertainment industry in particular, I've dealt with people who possessed many different types of personalities. Interestingly enough, the most common personality that I came across was the aggressive one.

Now, this industry is all about power and who knows who, so people walk around seeking to gain respect so that they will be seen as powerful people. It's almost like a tradition to walk around a movie studio lot and see the grips talk aggressively and shout at one another to get the job done. They don't take the abrasive nature of their rapport personally for the most part, but at the same time, when someone is having a bad day, these types of interactions may not go well. This is one of the reasons why there is such a high turnover rate in the industry, which is all of the aggression to get things done. But guess what? The aggressive boss is well respected by his employees, that's for sure, especially since most of his people are afraid of getting fired.

I can say, I've seen many relationships operate based on aggressive communication, in which one party is being intimidated by the one speaking to them. This type of issue usually results in argumentative

Finding Purpose

statements such as "If you don't act right, then I'm out." In one sense, communicating this way could mean that you're gaining respect from the person you're speaking with, but are you gaining their love? When you have people on your team who are there to help you fulfill your purpose, speaking with an emphasis on love helps. That said, the aggressive communicator usually speaks with much arrogance, mistaken by confidence.

Say we are at a press conference while making our comeback, and someone asks us, "So why are you choosing to make your comeback and fulfill your purpose?" And you respond with, "Because I can. I'm the man. Why do you want to know so bad?" The reporter would probably say, "Uh, I was just asking," and turn his microphone away.

Now you have gained a version of the respect you wanted, but you'll probably be on the paparazzi show later this evening, receiving a psychoanalysis of your erratic behavior. People would pick you apart. Think of people who were aggressive in their press conference, who had to come back and apologize to win back their fans. Most people don't care to support those who are constantly aggressive because it makes them seem arrogant as if they don't need their fans. This can also come from the "I've got this" attitude when a celebrity uses their aggression to express their seemingly high opinion of themselves.

Some people say extreme moments call for extreme measures, although I never recommend aggression as a form of healthy communication, even though we are all human. We will slip sometimes out of anger, or passion, but aggression should not be practiced consciously unless it is for true protection, meaning that if you are in real danger. Aggressive communication has a counterproductive, long-term effect, and if you use this technique, just know there may be follow-up consequences. For instance, there will likely be a lack of connection and love in your relationship, though, you may likely gain some form of respect.

The Passive Communicator is Loved by Many, Respected by Few

Remember the sweet girl in high school who was so fragile and nice? Everyone loved her. Or, what about the nice guy who was called a "sweetheart" by so many ladies. This is the last thing most men want to be, a sweetheart. There is one reason why, and you may already know what it is. The "nice guy" is loved by all of the ladies, but none of them respect him enough to give him a shot at a real relationship, or even a fun date out on the town. Don't get me wrong, ladies love guys who can be nice, but not "nice" guys.

Many men these days even go to the extreme of putting on the front of having this outgoing, demanding personality. An example of this phenomenon would be reality television star "The Situation" from MTV's immensely popular show *Jersey Shore*. Men like him will tell a lady, "Let's go out. I don't care if you're busy, cancel it." It's strange but true that many ladies will respect his approach at the beginning of establishing a romantic connection and say, "Ok." Of course, many will oppose it, but that type of aggressive demand does get respect. If you notice, connections that start on those kinds of terms will often times ends up in those same women saying, "I hate that guy."

Remember, the aggressor is often respected but rarely loved. But the passive guy would normally walk up to the lady and ask, "Hey Kim, you look very nice today, but I mean that in a respectful way, Kim, would you like to hang out Friday night?" The response usually goes something like this, "Ah, thank you so much, but I have to wash my

Finding Purpose

shoes this Friday." The passive communicator is typically a non-effective communicator when it comes to something they want.

Being a passive communicator can work to one's advantage at times when one knows how to use it. I've seen many salesmen use the passive communication technique to sell cars and other products successfully. One salesman walked up to me while I was looking to purchase a vehicle and said, "That's a nice car you're checking out there, let me know if you want to see the inside." I thought, "Ok, he's not being pushy, and he's not showing desperation, so this may be a good car."

I then asked him, "What's great about this car, and why should I purchase a vehicle from here, what kind of perks do I get with it?" He said, "Well, it's a pretty good car, and we're just another decent dealership who treats their customers well. There are others out there like us, but not many."

Now I was really confused and thinking, "Why isn't he trying to sell this to me? I'd hate to walk away from it, and he sells it to the next guy." It was almost frustrating that he wasn't being typical, but his passive attitude made me even more curious about the product.

Now, here and there, a man may approach a young lady, and if he knows how to be passive, and looks like he has a strong confident backbone, he may build her curiosity and gain her interest. This is what I call being a "balanced communicator."

Back to making that "comeback announcement." You may find a way to communicate passively if that's your personality, but it is still important to show them your firmness and seriousness, and as they build curiosity in your journey, they will want to be a part of it.

Finding Purpose

The Well Balanced Mutual Communicator Knows
When to Convince, Knows how to Gain Respect, and is Loved by Many

In speaking about many types of communicators and techniques in communication, it makes sense to speak in the most effective form there is possible. First off, we should understand the importance of being an effective communicator. What does being effective actually mean? This means being a communicator who hears and understands what's being said to them – the task that is generally known as listening – and one who speaks a message that is understood and received as sincere. Though each form of communication has its benefits and drawbacks, we must know when to use them and when to combine them, in order to not only deliver our message but to preserve our relationships with those we are speaking to. If the relationship is not important to preserve, why are we speaking to those people anyway?

The first important factor in performing effective communication with someone is knowing the personality of the person you are dealing with. So many people make the mistake of having the "accept me for who I am" attitude, having the thought that someone should adjust themselves to you, as you're trying to make your point. That's forgetting the big picture, particularly when someone else wants to express themselves as well. The big picture is being able to ultimately get your point across.

If someone is offended by what you say, you're not getting your point across, you're just saying something offensive. For example, if you're trying to influence someone to sell you something before their boss gets in and you are not being assertive, you may end up walking home empty-handed. Take time out to understand the personality of the person you're trying to get your message across to. In some cases, that means you may have to step out of your comfort zone to be effective. This is because not everyone will respond to your default personality in the same way.

Even more, than you feeling comfortable in your own communication, it is important for the person you're interacting with to feel comfortable receiving your message. Even if your disposition is aggressive, I wouldn't yell at some meek lady who appears to have fragile feelings, just to convince her to work harder in her position on a job. If you're dealing with someone who is very assertive, and you're trying to inspire them in a business meeting to increase sales, I would not recommend speaking passively, but assertively and passionately. When your mate comes home from work, and you're upset because you want to address an issue, I wouldn't speak to your spouse aggressively, but with a mixture of a little assertiveness and a little passiveness.

It is wise to practice combining forms of communication according to who we're speaking to, and how they appear to feel at the moment. Though there will be times to eliminate certain forms of communicating according to who you're speaking with, there is a part of communication that should never be eliminated in any conversation: listening. Remember that when you're standing at the microphone saying, "I'm back!" It is a good thing to listen to your fans as they voice their passionate constructiveness while you start your journey, for it tells them, "You matter". You're telling your fiancé, "You matter," you're telling your mother, "You matter," and you're telling your friends, "You matter."

Here are some suggestions to practice when engaging in a conversation with someone to be more effective:

Finding Purpose

- » What is their personality? Examples: meek, quiet, outgoing, thick skin, sensitive, etc.
- » What type of mood are they in? Examples: tired, frustrated, uplifted, relaxed, tensed, etc.
- » What message do I want to get across?
- » How should I express it, according to all of the above?
- » And last but not least, listen.
- » Once you have implemented these practices, you will be a great and effective communicator.

Chapter Four

Rob O' Brien's Reflection

What Does Purpose Mean to Me... By Rob O'Brien

When I reflect on what "purpose" means to me, the question, "why am I here?" comes to my consciousness. This power and the relevance of this question are limitless. I could continue to ask this question forever. The older I get and the more life experience I have, I understand how this question is constantly evolving.

I believe we are drawn to many different purposes in our life and they often build upon each other to create our next purpose. Sometimes we could be drawn to what we are innately good at and sometimes we can gravitate to things that we are challenged or intrigued by and, as a result, we learn immensely through the process.

Is what I am naturally good at actually what I am meant to do? Do I have a choice? Is my purpose predestined? How do I know if I am aligned with my purpose? What does my purpose look like? These are some questions I have often pondered during my 40 years.

Before I was old enough to make a choice to play hockey, my father laced up some skates and put me on the ice at age 3. I had barely

Finding Purpose

learned how to walk and now I had to navigate these awkward boots with sharp blades. As I got older I grew to love the sport and I started to excel in it. Hockey became my life. A sport I initially never made a conscious decision about all of a sudden became my purpose. I was convinced that I was destined to be a professional hockey player.

Just as it is with most young boys who dream of a career as a professional athlete, my dream never did come to fruition. It's something I now see as a good thing, considering I still have my teeth and never suffered a concussion.

Of course, we have a choice with our purpose. We have a choice with everything in life. That is one of the amazing gifts we have in life. Even though, getting stuck in the concept of trying to make the "right" choice can often occur and the thoughts can say, "What if it doesn't work out?" Certainly, we can be our own worst critics.

I believe we all have many purposes, great and small. Are they predestined? Maybe. But everyone is different and we all have different desires and likes and dislikes. We are all programmed differently. I remember personally training a client a few years back. She was a school teacher. I asked her how was it that she knew she wanted to be a school teacher. She told me that whenever she walked into a school, she would breathe it in and just loved the smell of any school.

Though seemingly simple, I thought that was such an amazing response. She had found something that she innately wanted to do, and it actually tickled her senses to the point of happiness. Certainly, that scenario did not resonate with my experience of walking into a school, which is usually followed by a gag reflex.

Using my schoolteacher client as evidence, we are aligned with our purpose when we felt alive and connected. It is something that feels natural at the moment. Almost like everything that brought us to this was intricate and complex, but at the same time easy and effortless.

I have asked for feedback in my past about my purpose, which has always been very useful and helpful, but trusting in our own inner guidance is often the most beneficial. It's true that sometimes learning and hearing others' perspectives can guide us to our own inner answers. And that is the point right there. The answers are all within us already.

All purposes are unique to the individual, so they look completely different from one person to another. We can learn through the journey of other people telling about the process of their purpose, but ultimately we are all creators and we are all different and special in our own way.

Thus I can learn through others' journeys as they seek their purpose, but ultimately my purpose has a story that unravels very differently than even my best friends, mom, or sisters. Also as I go on the journey of a purpose in my life, I actually do not know what has happened until I take a step back, reflect and process everything.

What is my Purpose?

The eternal question! As I coach clients in my life coaching business, I try not to give them advice, but rather to guide people in helping them recognize what already resides within them. When I am searching for my own inner answers, I reflect within. Then I reach out to people that I trust, to give me feedback. That allows me to assess and access what is true or valid for me. I do not want someone's advice on my situation based on their beliefs or life because it will inevitably always be different. We are all unique and are individuals and have special things that we want to create.

Finding Purpose

I believe in my 40 years on this earth, I have chosen jobs that were right for me at certain times because they propelled me to get me to the next place in my life.

When I was 20 and in college, I became drawn to the physical body. I played sports all of my life and was still playing in college. I started to lift weights to make myself stronger, but I was fascinated with the science about how that works. So I engulfed myself in exercise physiology, reading everything on the subject.

I must admit other stuff I was reading was Arnold Schwarzenegger's "Encyclopedia on Bodybuilding" as well as all the countless trendy bodybuilding magazines and books of the day in the mid-'90s. Some things worked and some were bogus, and all were walking contradictions. But the reason they were contradictions was the simple fact that what works for one person certainly doesn't always work for another. We all have different body types and genetics, etc. So I would spend hours in the gym and go nowhere.

It wasn't until I started to experiment with different training tactics that my growth began. Instead of training for two hours a day, I trained for forty-five minutes and only trained one body part per week instead of three times per week. I didn't realize that these magazines that were giving me advice were from bodybuilders that had freaky genetics and were possibly taking performance-enhancing drugs.

My passion for the body manifested in wanting to teach others how to train correctly and efficiently. I wanted to tell them my mistakes and help them save time and energy in getting the body they desired or reaching the goal they aspired to. I got certified as a personal trainer and started training clients.

Finding Purpose

After about ten years of personal training, I realized that one could only get someone to their physical goals so far. I was essentially a therapist to my clients, talking about their aspirations and their fears and what was keeping them from reaching their goals and the life they wanted in the current moment.

Ironically, through listening to them, I was also learning about myself. I wanted to do something more than simply train people about their physical bodies. I wanted to coach them on their entire beings. And so the universe led me to pursue a graduate degree in Spiritual Psychology.

The word "spiritual" can scare people, as we often associate the word with religion, which may have a reaction. When people would ask me what Spiritual Psychology was, I simplified it by saying, "It is getting to the root of all that is blocking you from having the life you want."

Through my two-year Master's program, I experienced all the irrational beliefs that I had acquired. I looked within to why I was repeating certain patterns in my life, how those patterns were affecting me, and, once at that awareness, how I could work to let them go and reframe things so I would not sabotage myself from reaching my goals. Essentially it was working at being aware of the ego, acknowledging that it is there, and accepting it, rather than pushing it away. I adopted their frame for the ego as, "Edge God Out." Now I am always asking myself if whatever I am going through is coming from my ego or my true self?

After graduate school, I started my own life coaching business. I call it Core Intention. Everything stems from the core and what we put our attention on is what manifests in our life. I currently still have my life coaching practice, which is always evolving as I change and grow. After all, the base of EVOLve and EVOLution is love spelled backwards, which to me means going back to the one foundation we all have within, which is Love.

However, three years ago, I was led to a line of work that combines my awareness of the physical body, as well as my knowledge of the analytical mind, along with my connection with the spiritual self and my experience of the emotional attachment of desires. We all are aware of all of these phenomena to varying degrees, but we usually are better or focus more on a couple of them rather than cultivating all of them from within.

I work at a place called "The Genius of Flexibility," which combines the physical, mental, emotional, and spiritual work I have done in the past, all together. All the work I have done has gotten me to this point in my life to do the work I am doing now. And, I am certain the work I am doing now is preparing me for my next endeavor.

As we evolve and change, so does our purpose and our life expression. And it all builds on one another.

If someone were to ask me, how they can find their purpose, I would first say, instead of looking outside of yourself for the answer, take some time to reflect and turn within. Write down all that you love to do. I guarantee this will be different for everybody. Put it on your refrigerator or somewhere where you can view it to remind yourself of all the things you love to do.

Then create an ideal scene of your purpose, using active language, such as, "I am waking up every morning excited to embrace the day and express myself to the world through my current life's work." But be really specific and see where it takes you. I have created many ideal

Finding Purpose

scenes for my career and relationships and often I have put them aside, only then to revisit them months later and realize that everything I wrote down, I manifested in my life.

Intention is a powerful thing. What we put our intention and attention on is what we create in our life. Our outer world and circumstances are simply a reflection of what is residing and present inside of us. If I do not like my current circumstances and what is going on around me, then I have an opportunity to reassess and make the necessary adjustments and changes that are more in alignment with what I want.

We are all responsible for ourselves and have the ability to create, be, and do whatever we want. When we become victims to blaming others or the outside world for our circumstances, then we give away our God-given power.

Let's all take back our power, search within, and get clarity on what we individually love to do and what we want to create, and how we want to put a stamp on this world. If we all do it, this world will be a magnificent place, filled with individual creations, all unique and special in their own way, coming together as one.

The more I learned that the life challenges, circumstances, trauma, and drama I had brought into my life by always saying I am a survivor or I can survive any situation, only created more challenges and situations to deal with. I didn't understand why other people had it so easy or so much less heartache? I thought I was cursed. - April Peebles

Chapter Five

STEP 3. DEALING WITH FEAR AND ANXIETY

NOTES

Dealing with Fear and Anxiety:
Massaging the "not" out of – I cannot Face this Challenge

Over the next few chapters, we will be exploring the PTA – People Tools Action System.

Below is a Prioritization Chart which lays out goals, beginning at the top with #1 as the highest priority, down to the bottom with #5. The idea of this triangular-shaped chart is to express how we prioritize space in our lives for our goals.

With this chart, in particular, we have goal #1 features as the section we provide the most space for when working towards success, and in #5, we provide the least space in our lives to work towards that goal.

Naturally, even if we are not intentionally dividing our time unequally towards accomplishing several tasks, we are always prioritizing some goals over others, and devoting more time, strategy, and energy towards only some of our objectives.

Here we have the foundation of PTA: goal setting. Write down your list of goals for today, with #1 being the highest priority. This goal could be focused on your career, education, your favorite hobby, or whatever you would like for it to be. Once you have 3 to 5 goals listed, we will take the first goal, and we will use that goal to practice the PTA system throughout the rest of this book. The small triangles at the corner of the main goal chart are where a list of people, tools, and action steps that can help you achieve your goals will be described.

Prioritization Chart - Goals

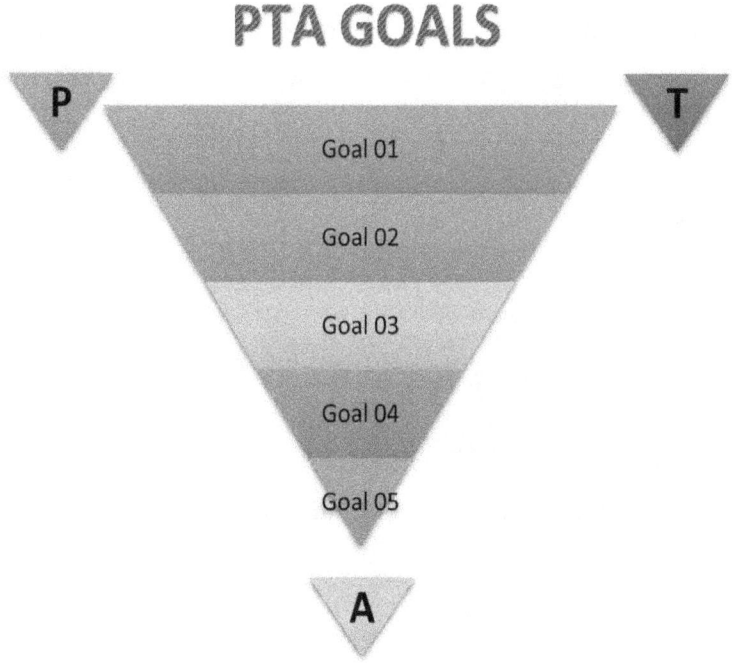

Accepting the Reality of What's Coming

When you're in the mood for sweets, and you're not good at following recipes, once your warm, double chocolate chip cookies come out of the oven, your significant other may taste them and say, "That's one tough cookie". That's not a good thing to hear in that sense, but in our case, the same comment wouldn't be about our chocolate chip cookies. Instead, we're talking about people. I've always told young guys growing up who are constantly trying to prove themselves through competition to show their toughness, that being tough isn't about what you can do but what you can handle.

If you're walking the streets and you jump on a group of guys and beat them up, you just won a selected fight, but this doesn't mean that you're tough. On the contrary, if you're walking down the street and a group of guys jump on you, and you lose, and you're willing to walk down that same street tomorrow with precaution, that's what makes you tough. Winning is based on standing your ground, not just on taking the bout.

Otherwise, Bill Gates would be considered a loser, because I'm sure he's had more than a few failed attempts before he was able to design software and actually get it developed and distributed successfully. But by him standing his ground in believing he was the best software designer around, he was still able to design some of the best software with confidence because his failures did not represent his potential or his worth.

As celebrities start working toward making their comeback after falling off the map, they should understand everything that will come with it. Yes, this includes the good, but also the bad. The tabloids will start running after them while they're on vacation, jogging at the beach

Finding Purpose

in Hawaii. Internet sources will take snapshots focusing on their physical flaws, and speak about them harshly. There will be people clinging to them, seeming sincere, but just wanting to receive a piece of their comeback fame, until they're not in the spotlight anymore. So why would they sacrifice a portion of their peace and privacy in order to make their comeback anyway? Because what they stand to gain is a lot better than what they have to sacrifice.

I was speaking to a young teenage girl about bringing her academics up in school after she had missed about a month. She said the reason for her missing so many classes were because of issues she was dealing with at home, and she finally started giving up on life because of the stress she dealt with daily. She started sinking into an academic hole, and before she knew it, she was deeper than she could imagine digging herself out of.

As most problems in life are temporary, so were the conflicts that she was dealing with at home. Fortunately, things between her and her parents eventually became better. That was a good thing, but now she still had to deal with the problem of her grades that had fallen.

I asked her what her plans were forgetting her grades up. At that point, she had started leaving school from feeling too overwhelmed since her scores had fallen so low. I immediately asked her about her future plans in life, and what she wanted to become. She stated that wanting to receive her business management degree after high school was a major goal of hers. I asked her if she would be willing to allow a month of catching up in class to prevent her from enjoying a lifetime of benefitting from working in the business world? She said no. She realized the sacrifice of focusing would take a lot of work, but that the benefits of a lifetime of enjoyment would be worth it. She realized that in her situation, the gain would be better than the sacrifice. The young girl ended up going back to school and developed a plan with her teachers and counselors to bring her grades up. She even convinced them of how serious she was, which inspired them greatly to assist her, and once she devoted herself to her academic plan, it worked.

The Undefeated Team is On the Way – Accepting the Reality

Can you remember a time, if you've either played a sport or had someone close to you playing one when you were about to face the most challenging team of the season's schedule? The team was either undefeated or close to it. If you have, then you know that throughout the time leading up to the game, there would be a lot of talk and study about how to best approach competing with this team in question.

When I played football, years ago, and we played a challenging team, we would always throw off that team by doing something different against the team than the way we had played against other teams. The reality we had to accept was the fact that the team we had to play could arguably be the best in the league, and thus we had to do something other than usual to beat them.

We would consider the size of the challenge we were facing, especially since we knew that our usual business would not be good enough. We also accepted the reality that this team was on their way to play this game with the express intention of beating us. Knowing this, we stood bold and confident, accepting what they wanted to do. By accepting this reality, we were better able to prepare to defeat them, or simply gain victory from how we handled the situation. The one thing we did not do was run from them, or forfeit the game. We had too many friends and family to let down, not to mention ourselves, whom we had to face as well.

Finding Purpose

Many times we can even look at life's challenges the same way as the big game. The bigger the challenge is, the bigger the victory. How would you prep for the biggest game of the season? Wouldn't you have the biggest pep rally of the year? The cheerleaders would do the biggest stunts of the year, just like you would do the most studying of the year. The bottom line is, when you're facing your biggest challenges, it calls for the most preparation.

Dealing with Fear and Anxiety

In track and field, people used to say, when you have anxiety, it means you're going to have a good race. What they meant was this: when you're in an anxious state of mind, your mind is usually working at its maximum capacity to utilize everything it knows about what you're facing. It is normal to feel some anxiety at the moment of being in the spotlight, but we can't let it rule our minds and emotions.

In these types of situations, we must find a way to keep our anxiety under control. The better we are prepared for an action, the more it will usually lessen the anxiety we feel to face that action. All we can do is our best at the moment we are facing the challenge while making sure that it is our best when we're doing it.

As another example in dating, there has always been an issue I've had to deal with to which I'm sure many others can also relate. The issue I'm talking about is transitioning from dating to the status of being in a relationship. Not that I didn't know how to make this happen, but when it was supposed to, I experienced the anxiety of what comes with being in a committed relationship. The good benefits were easy to deal with, like having someone to hang out with at group dinners. I would enjoy having someone to express my thoughts with when I wanted to share. It's great having someone to share your emotional burdens and highs with. But there is another component of relationships: the Challenges.

Expecting and Facing Common Relationship Issues

Years ago, the singer Usher had a song that said, "You remind me." He was speaking of a girl he dated in the past, which reminded him of a girl he was thinking of dating at the present time. He sang about the acknowledgement of why he was fearing the future possible relationship he was on the verge of committing to, because of bad encounters with a girl who had similar traits to the possible mate he was singing about. Have you been there before?

I'm sure there will be many traits of someone you have experienced in the past that may seem to show up in your new, developing relationships. The traits could even be good things of the past, but many times there are negative behaviors. I don't necessarily understand why, but it is something many of us do. We will tell ourselves to leave someone alone, and then go subconsciously seek out the same things in someone else. Though we are usually unconscious of the fact of us doing so, many times it does bring those fears to the surface.

"I wonder if her flirtation is going to result in her cheating on me as the last one did?" "I wonder if his impatience is going to cause him to leave me as the last one did?" These are questions we will ask ourselves when dealing with relationship fears that are rooted in our problems from the past. So we will take these connections to our past and start building bridges between ourselves and the person we are currently dating as a defense mechanism. We begin to shut down in a sense, hurting our chances to take part in a possibly healthy new relationship.

I've heard many people say fear stands for False Evidence Appearing Real. This means that we will see the false evidence of what

Finding Purpose

we have been through, and become convinced that we are going through our previous problems yet again. Like in business, we can say, "I started a business in the past, and it failed, so it will fail in the future". Just the same, we can say before a future job interview, "I've failed all of my previous management interviews, so I know I will fail this one in the future".

Fear is an emotion that will keep you stuck in a place that you don't want to be. Our past is not our future, but simply a collection of our experiences. If we learn from our experiences, we have moved one step closer to successfully accomplishing that thing that did not manifest successfully back then.

Is it Worth It?

One question I always ask before engaging in any activity is, is it worth it? Is it worth the time, the money, and/or the energy? In other words, it's got to make sense. When I'm teaching a workshop on any given topic, the one thing I emphasize is, sometimes we just have to go back to the basics.

For example, as it pertains to this section of the chapter, ask the simple question before getting involved in any situation: Is it worth it? How many times do we fight for a relationship that isn't going well, or fight a battle where there will clearly be no victory, or think about doing an activity you would regret as revenge on someone who made you upset without even asking if it's worth it?

When someone is making a comeback in a sport, or just in life in general, it has to be worth it. The worth is obviously in the benefits of taking on this task, in comparison to its possible risks or repercussions. If I decide to play football again, is it worth taking a risk of getting injured? Well, if I plan on getting a Super Bowl ring, maybe; or if I will get a feeling of accomplishment that will boost me in many other areas of my life, maybe; but not just to play.

The worth of what we do is in the purpose of what we are doing. In life, this is where we find our worth, in purpose. Our greatest accomplishment in life is finding our purpose. This is what drives us and keeps us motivated whenever we face adversity. When making that comeback in any area of your life, ask this question: what is my purpose? Then, connect to it. When times get tough, just saying I'm going to come back just to come back will not be good enough. You must connect to your purpose, or else you will surely collapse. Your purpose will answer the question, as you say: yes, this is worth it.

You can face this Challenge

Taking a leap of faith in life can mean anything from marrying your high school sweetheart to moving out of the house for the first time, or second, or third time. The point is, each time we make a major move in life, we are aware of the fact that there will be challenges we must face in order to gain success in that move.

When I first moved out of my parents' house, I knew I needed to maintain a job to pay my rent and buy food. In order to do so, I knew it would be wise to eventually purchase a vehicle to have more employment options as I would need a car to work at remote facilities. I also knew that getting in good with the manager of my building would save me if my rent was late or if I wanted to throw a late-night get-together here and there. I subconsciously implemented my PTA system: People Tools Actions.

In order to move successfully from home, I had to connect with people, acquire and utilize tools, such as a vehicle, and take action. I had to intelligently and effectively approach my moving out to make

Finding Purpose

the transition to my new home a success. This transition of moving out would cause temporary setbacks financially, and additional added pressures, but it would also increase my level of privacy and freedom. So, for one, I recognized that the setbacks and pressures would be worth the gain.

Once again, facing any challenge in life takes energy and some discomfort, but we become stronger through each challenge if we embrace the lessons we learn from each. As we become stronger, and with every challenge we face in our future, it becomes less difficult each time we are presented with it until we conquer it.

Challenges help us reach our fullest potential. Challenges force us to discover the best qualities that lie deep within us in order to succeed in a given task. With proper preparation, the task we face becomes less challenging, giving us less anxiety to deal with, and leaving our mind's capacity with a more available room for creativity in conquering what's before us.

When you have a final exam in school that you've prepared for endlessly, you walk in the classroom with confidence, saying in your mind, give me the test while the information is fresh. You are anticipating facing the test because you know the preparation you have put into it. You also know the importance of facing the challenge with what it takes to defeat it while your resources are still fresh. Preparation is the key.

When it's time to face a challenge, whether it's starting a clothing company, confronting a member of the family, or moving to a new home, ask yourself, is it worth it, even though you know you may have to live off of Top Ramen noodles for the next six months. In seeing its benefits as bigger than the sacrifice, you're acknowledging its purpose.

Finding Purpose

Once its purpose is defined, it is imperative that you connect with your disposition and confidently establish your anchor.

Enjoying the Benefits – Indulge Responsibly

Godiva chocolate-covered strawberries – that's all I have to say. They seem to taste better around Valentine's Day. Jambalaya with rice at the Cheesecake Factory, or fresh baked chocolate chip cookies at Ms. Fields. These are things that are so good, but yet so bad. When any of these temptations are present, I must indulge responsibly. I must enjoy the benefits in moderation, because I know the consequences of over-consuming, which is normally about two more inches in my waist. I know that too many cookies will give me a sugar high, and a major crash would soon follow, draining all of my energy.

When it's time to enjoy the benefits of our hard work, we must do it in moderation. Whether it's going into our favorite ice cream spot or going to the local bar for drinks and festivities, there are benefits and consequences to things that seem to be purely enjoyable, but require a considerable degree of restraint to benefit from in the most responsible way possible.

This is also true when receiving a paycheck at the end of two weeks for a job, we must know how to budget our money with bills, and that what's left will be considered our disposable income. But if we just blow the whole check, with no moderation, we might as well say goodbye to the car, or even worse, the house, since the bank would soon own it. This is how we keep control of ourselves, by indulging responsibly. It gives us a sense of how disciplined our lives really are when we are giving ourselves permission to do what we want.

When we are able to discipline ourselves in moderating pleasure, it's like our consciousness speaking to our physical being and saying, "I

Finding Purpose

am in control of you." As a result, when it's time to study for the big test, or practice the script for the upcoming play, or wake up a few hours before work to get your morning aerobics in, you have already begun training yourself to get something done, even when you don't feel like it. In life, we must train ourselves. We must get ourselves used to doing things we need to do when we don't feel like it, and also not doing things we shouldn't even when we may think we feel like doing it.

For one moment, think about something you really enjoy doing that causes no harm to you or other people. Now think about this. What if this thing began to take over your life, or valuable time, to where there wasn't any left for productivity? Any harmless thing can become a problem if it is indulged irresponsibly. So enjoy life, but do so in moderation. When it comes to how we manage food, spending, playing, working, or anything else we are into, and how we minimize the consequences of overindulging, it speaks to us in how disciplined our lives really are.

You have built yourself strong by preparing to face the challenge. You are confident in your soon-to-be victory and ready to make your move. Having the confidence to "Go for it" is a victory in itself, and this is cause for a small celebration!

Many people are defeated before the battle simply because they are not sure of how to dig deep within themselves and find that inner fire to face their challenge, or they are just simply not prepared mentally, physically, spiritually, and or emotionally to do so. Massage the "I cannot" out of your life and the way that you perceive things. Now the question that should remain is, what's my next move?

Finding Purpose

Once you have implemented these practices, you can face this challenge!

Chapter Six

April Peebles's Reflection

Finding Purpose in the now......just like you, I have had many ups and downs in my life. Most of my life was spent trying to climb out of a gigantic sinkhole that seemed to encapsulate me. I know some of you reading this can relate. Throughout my life, no matter how horrible the situation I found myself in, I always seemed to effortlessly bounce back ten times better than where I was when the trauma and drama in my life occurred.

Since I can remember, I hung onto the label and belief that I was a survivor. That is what my belief was about myself. I was here on this earth to SURVIVE, that life was bad and bad things were always going to happen to me. As I got older and went through the journey of my life, I got wiser and more educated with every experience I found myself in. I became addicted subconsciously to creating circumstances just so I could creatively get myself out of the situation. I felt like I had a superpower of some sort.

It was a type of adrenaline rush for me, and I didn't even realize I was doing this on a conscious level until I enrolled in school to become a certified Hypnotherapist. About nine years ago, I was given a movie called "The Secret" and this movie hit home for me. It really opened my eyes to what the power really was and how I was using it all wrong.

My first thought was confusion on why the school system never taught us this power? Why it would want to leave this amazing ability to create the life we all strive for. I really began faithfully practicing this law of attraction, and my world changed. Through watching this film, I began changing my life by changing my thoughts from negativity to positivity. I went from being a serial survivor to a creative "thriver."

The more I learned that the life challenges, circumstances, trauma, and drama I had brought into my life by always saying I am a survivor or I can survive any situation, only created more challenges and situations to deal with.

Do you ever find yourself thinking that you have a curse? Would you believe me if I told you that you really could, and you are doing it to yourself just by having that thought in your head? Our brains are living computers and they only operate on what we believe and hold to be true. The brain doesn't know the difference between real and make-believe, and therefore sends out signals to draw the things to you that you think about most. Believe it or not, everything you think or believe isn't always real....It's only real to you. That is why everyone has a different set of beliefs and morals and values.

All I did was create more situations to survive with my thoughts. I would always say WHAT's next, or NOW what, or bring it on. And as sure as I thought -- and, most of the time, yelled -- these words out loud to the universe or god, something more would come into my life that would cause drama, trauma, and more upset to enter my already unstable world.

Finding Purpose

When nothing was going on and things were seemingly going well, I found ways unconsciously to sabotage my peace and happiness. My belief was that I could trust no one, and guess what popped into my life? People who mistreated me.

They were my thoughts that were attracting those types of people into my life over and over. Because of how personal experiences affected me, this misbelief followed me throughout my life.

Obviously, there were many good people in my life, but some of them never had a fair chance. I was programmed to believe that most people would eventually hurt me. That is what I expected, and that is what I was used to, as this bad programming was me operating on an old belief; I was only able to change this belief once I was able to release it and let it go.

My children are the ones who held me down, to live in my ultimate purpose. They keep me grounded, literally and figuratively. They have allowed me to live in the now, opposed to living in a life of searching and striving for one ultimate goal. I know where my ultimate purpose is, but am I there yet? NO! Do I have an idea of what this ultimate purposeful life looks like? Yes. I can see it, feel it, and it is in my future.

Every day I know that, although I am operating in the now, I am working toward this ultimate achievement in my life. I have found that through living in the moment, I am able to be blessed with finding more than one purpose in my life. A part of my purpose for this world was to have my children so that they could live out their purpose, so mine just grew multiple times, by being a mother. My purpose for them is to change the world one person at a time, starting with them. I will teach them to live a life of following the rules but living in the gray and staying out of the black and white. To test boundaries without

Finding Purpose

breaking the law, and to see outside the boxes of education, religion, and most of all social standards.

Don't follow the herd. Stand out, stand for something, and never ever build a future for someone else. I will teach them to be different and to be proud of their differences, and never to compare themselves to others. To not let standardized testing at school define them as human beings, and to never lose their imagination, original creativity, or intuition and, yet still, allow me to live a purposeful life.

Living purposefully in the "Now" allows you to find peace, joy, and happiness. If you're always thinking reflecting and holding on to the past you will find that you are most likely depressed, unhappy, stuck in a rut, and not moving forward in life. If you are constantly worried about your future, you will find that you are constantly stressed out and living with anxiety and sometimes fear of the unknown.

I have been able to find harmony and a level of peace in my life by balancing out the past, present, and future to create a foundation of which I know that no matter what, God will provide for me and that all things that happen are for a reason.

If I can't change my situation I adjust my wings and I fly with the direction of the wind until I find that actually is the thing that gives me the most strength and momentum in my life, and sends me in the direction I need to be going. Sometimes things happen in life and we don't always understand it and that is what is so funny about life. It really only makes sense to us when we look back on it.

Purpose to me isn't one thing that has to be fulfilled at one given moment or at one time. Purpose, in my life, showed up after many, many countless wasted years of trying to find myself only to lose myself

Finding Purpose

more and more with each self-help book and YouTube motivation speech I watched. It was only after digging into my darkest fears, and all the ugliest sides of myself that even I was afraid to face, that I was able to truly discover who I was. After all, you are only able to be the best version/ person of your worst self.

Looking in the mirror and not liking who I was (or was not, for that matter) although I was not sure which one frightened me more, I was able to come to the conclusion that finding my purpose was not at all about discovering and finding me. It was about finding my purpose so that I would finally arrive at the best version of me because your purpose isn't about who you are it is who you become in the process.

For so long I was lost, and I thought it was because I was lost, but the reality is that I am ME. You can't lose yourself. I was never lost as a soul or a person, but rather in an ocean of purpose that was yet to be discovered. I was here for a reason, and not knowing that reason was keeping me focused on the passion of finding myself rather than finding my purpose. So if you're reading this – which you are – and you can relate to being on the tireless journey of looking for YOURSELF, then I strongly urge you to stop and start focusing on finding your purpose rather than yourself.

I always thought that if I figured out who I was that I could be and find happiness. But as many years passed – almost 33 to be exact – I was the opposite of happiness. I was in the worst place of my life. My life had turned life upside down and inside out. I was the most creative, passionate, empathic, loving, giving, unselfish, a vulnerable person I knew, but looking in the mirror I felt that all those traits had been taken advantage of so many times that I had developed walls that were the opposite of who I was at my core. The woman in the mirror was

Finding Purpose

angry, hateful, unmotivated, lost, unlovable, selfish, and the most closed off.

Most people have been slapped into submission and taught at an early age to not become what they are passionate about but to be what we are taught we have to be, not visionaries but robots. It is hard to get out of the box that society puts us in starting at a pre-K level. We give our kids to the government at age four, but in return, do they teach them values about loving others, themselves, or how to be passionate and compassionate? They teach them to test.

I once saw an image of animals that were all being tested on climbing a tree, and then graded on that. Imagine an elephant climbing a tree. The monkey passed with flying colors but just what if the test was on carrying logs….the elephant would have passed and the monkey would have failed. This is the belief system that is instilled in our children which, if you fail, you are a failure. You begin to believe this about yourself instead of a system that allows your child to truly discover who they are.

We could create tests that guide them to their passion and their purpose, and to teach them that we are all here to do different things. It is your job to help them get in touch with their imagination. Teach your kids to hold onto the things that give them dreams, and encourage imagination because that is where creativity flows from which is where we invent and create lives that are worth living. If you can see it, believe it, and you can achieve it.

When my oldest son was born, he changed the entire shape of my future. No longer was my future what I had planned out in my head to be. While I was pregnant, I quickly found myself thrown into a world of unknowns and struggles.

Finding Purpose

No test in school prepared me for this moment in my life which meant I would possibly have to raise a child with a minimum wage income. No one told me what to do, I had to start thinking outside the box to survive, and that is where I began discovering that this was a blessing. I was able to break free from society's expectations and the boxes that I had been put into. I was now going to have to do things backwards, which seemed to be the hard way. I had to work three jobs. Things seemed overwhelming and I hardly ever saw my son because he was always in someone else's care, so that I could seemingly provide for him.

Boy was this backwards.

Purpose gives meaning to our lives so that every area – whether in our family, academics, and even jobs – becomes fulfilling.
– Johnathan Kendrick

Chapter Seven

Step 4. Connecting to People Tools Action

NOTES

Connecting to People Tools Action – PTA System: Massaging the "not" out of – I cannot Maintain Healthy Relationships

I'm sure you've overheard someone say at one time or another, "I have connections." This is because people understand the importance of knowing people who are connected to the thing that they want to accomplish the most, but many of us don't utilize those same people when the opportunity presents itself. The fact is, most of us are not building those connections as we go about our everyday activities. I tell people in my workshops that there is no such thing as "little people". Everyone has the same potential to become highly influential, rich, powerful, or any of those high levels of status in society, so just because an associate is struggling now does not mean you won't need them someday.

Finding Purpose

I have a few friends in the entertainment industry who are pretty successful, but I specifically want to talk about my friend Kevin. There was a time when Kevin and I would hang out on the weekends, and any time during the week when we were not working or had any other obligations. I would go over to his house and hang with him and his roommate doing anything from producing music together, to writing scripts, to talking and laughing about our encounters with different people throughout that week.

Kevin was struggling financially, as was I at the time, but he didn't allow that to change him. Many of his friends seemed to be picking up momentum in their careers and growing financially, but it seemed like he was stuck as a struggling actor. I remember Kevin calling some of his other buddies, trying to organize some catching-up time with them. They, all of a sudden, seemed to be busy all of the time, saying things like "Oh, man, I have to work, I'm not sure if I can make it." Then he had other friends who would say, "What's up? Yeah, I'll meet you at the restaurant on Saturday," but for some reason, they wouldn't show up. Not only that, but they wouldn't even return his calls for up to a week, even after flaking on their previous appointments to hang out and get something to eat.

Kevin, being the positive guy he is, would make excuses at first, saying things like, "Man, he forgot again." There was one incident where Kevin and I, along with some other buddies, were planning a trip to Catalina Island for a day with some lady friends. Kevin's lady gave him a call the day before saying, "I have to do something with my sister, sorry, I won't be able to make it." I can understand there are incidents where people have to bail out of situations because of unexpected circumstances, but it seemed this was a curse that Kevin was stuck with.

As time went by, and his friends fell off one by one, Kevin's debts grew deeper and deeper, and the reality began to set in as to why his popularity had become a thing of the past. He realized that his friends had sunk to a new low by judging him for his lack of income stability due to unfortunate circumstances he was going through financially.

Kevin eventually became bitter, saying things like, "I'm done with people, I'm just going to focus on me." It seemed like he started sinking his head into a shell, cutting himself off from the world. The effect this had on him was that Kevin began to lose his connections for opportunities to open up for him, and his personality started changing into someone, not even he could recognize after a while. He became a totally different person.

When Kevin went to his acting auditions, he didn't seem as outgoing as he once was. His family began to see him as being distant. His boss on his day job said that his attitude had shifted to being negative, and Kevin started taking it personally. I had a talk with Kevin and told him a story I read of a man who seemed to have the world working against him. In my story, that guy didn't address the world not wanting to be involved with him, but he just kept his personality and kindness consistent as those people as he acquired success.

The man in the story said, "When there are negative or unsupportive people around you, don't address them, just be yourself around them." He also said, "Eventually, those people will see your progress in life, and though it may not be important to you, they will want to be on your team". He said, "The average person, sad to say, focuses on hanging with friends that can take them somewhere or

Finding Purpose

someone, and who can obviously give them something. Those, of course, are not genuine behaviors, but most people subconsciously do it."

This man said, "Do not make the same mistake as so many people do, which is changing as an individual, or turning those non-supportive people into enemies, by denouncing them." He said, "The ones who come around one day will be the ones who boost your career by purchasing tickets to your movies, or bragging about how they know you." This man said, "Keep the ball in your court."

I thought about this story when it had been told to me and it had changed my whole perspective on people, so I felt that it was necessary to pass it along to Kevin. After having this conversation with Kevin, he took my advice. Though people were not being supportive of him, he went back to his old outgoing self. People started wondering how he did it, keeping in mind that they had not returned his calls. They became curious about what he was up to. His acting auditions became even more explosive because he wouldn't allow studio executives to intimidate him. He acquired the confidence in not letting others dictate his character by how much they seemed to like him or wanted to be around him.

Kevin began to land jobs and pick up momentum in his life. After landing a few commercials and independent films, Kevin made it to the Big Screen. Guess what happened next? Yep, those friends who he once could not contact anymore began looking him up. They went out and purchased tickets to his movies, bought his DVD, and promoted him to everyone they knew. They became fans. The sad part on their end was this: he had already attracted a more committed base of supportive friends and associates, so he wasn't able to reach back to those older associates who once said they were buddies.

Guess what a few of them said, though, from his past? "Kevin changed, he's not as cool as he used to be. He turned Hollywood, and won't return my messages." They somehow forgot that they were the ones who originally lost contact. Even though they had these feelings about Kevin as he gained success, they spent much of their time talking about him to their friends and family, constantly seeking a reconnection to him. Kevin never turned them into enemies, so they became fans, and those people would eventually end up thinking about Kevin and tell their friends, "I've got connections."

It is important to keep in contact with those who have high ambition even if they are not where they want to be at that particular moment. Once again, we may need them someday. It is also important to constantly make new connections as we go about our lives each day because most opportunities come from who we know. We are talking about the importance of connecting to people, and how this can boost our level of success in all that we do.

Do you know people who are on social networking sites with over 1000 friends, but it seems like they have more free time on their hands than they want? They say on the weekend, "I'm bored," or they say, "Wow, I have not been able to find a job in over a year."

Are they serious? What are those people for on their friends list? They shouldn't just be decorations to help you feel important. There should be purpose in those relationships, even if they are shallow. Now some of these people's purpose can be to just be friends, or family, but most of us really don't have 1000 true friends. Many of those people are associates, but they can also be supporters, or we can become supporters of them. How can we turn every relationship that is connected to us into a purposeful association? That is the question.

KNOWING PEOPLE'S POSITION IN OUR LIFE

The Human Authority

As we are setting out to achieve something great that will require supporters to be a true success, we must establish our human authority. Our human authority is validation for what we are doing. It is our authenticity.

When someone is running for President, they start a campaign. In the campaigning, the candidate is trying to convince the people that they have what it takes to lead them to a better life. In order to convince them they can be the right leader, they must convince the voters of the authority that they can wield in the high positions of the political arena, the business world, and other areas of importance. This type of message will say to the people, "I can make it happen with my authority."

Another important factor in establishing human authority is letting people know that you are acting from a sincere place. For instance, when Barack Obama was running for President and speaking on healthcare reform, he referred to his mother who had passed away from cancer, and the limited options he had when she was in need of healthcare services. This was a connected, personal reason for him to want to implement healthcare reforms. Whether or not you supported his policies, his approach explained his motives to people before they could assume what they were.

In our human authority, we are not forcing anything on anyone, and thus not everyone will accept our position in establishing human authority. Though that is true, in expressing our human authority, we are attempting to convince people we are worthy of their support, and it also gives them a personal human experience to connect with as you seek to gain their support. You want people to say, "yes, I can connect with him/her."

Building a Fan Base for the Come Back

Everyone wants to be connected to something great. Why not be the "great" thing that they are connecting to? One of the biggest mistakes that happen in particular to the common person is we put too many restrictions and qualifiers on our connections. For instance, we feel everyone that we are connected to should be in one of only four categories: our family, friends, associates, or enemies.

In the celebrity world, think about Johnny Depp. If you like him as an actor, which one of those four categories would you say he fits in? Probably none. What if Johnny Depp said in an interview, "Hey, if I don't know you, you're not important." Or if he said to his fans, "Blood is thicker than water." Though he may feel this way, by saying it, he would be turning off his fans by making them feel disconnected from him. There are some people who just want to be connected to us in life, and it is wise to let them feel that they are, especially since it likely won't cause any harm.

There are many ways to burn bridges with people in our present and past. Say you've received an opportunity to work for someone, or if someone has already worked for you and they were a benefit to you. Now that person is reaching out to you for encouragement or advice, or just to say hello. If you become unavailable to them, it sends a message to the person, especially if they don't receive any kind of acknowledgement or explanation. The message you are sending

Finding Purpose

basically says, "You're not important." As you should know, this can create bitter feelings in what was once a beneficial connection. I encourage people to return your emails when you can or at least inform people on why you may not be able to get back to them with a fully invested response. Say I am swamped with messages and it is taking too much time to get back to everyone. It would make sense for me to tell them that if I don't get back to them, it's nothing personal, I'm just a little overwhelmed right now. But don't ignore them, because when you do, you may not be able to avoid burning that bridge.

Bridges are not just important for those who have the upper hand at that moment, but for those who are supporting that upper hand. It is impossible to achieve greatness if no one will support you in doing so. That person who has the, say, lower hand, maybe someone in a position to hire you someday when you're in need. They may become the CEO of a corporation or an established movie producer who can give you that first legitimate acting job. Never see anyone as unimportant, because no one is unimportant. Many times, we just have to find their purpose in our lives.

Dealing with Dream Killers

This is a sensitive area for many, and one that is so important in our journey to success, and that is dealing with the dream killers or the haters. Some people say if you can't beat 'em, join 'em. Well, it can be truly counterproductive to join the dream killers. This is how so many people sabotage their own dreams; they become their own dream killers.

We must be great judges of how to handle the dream killers that we encounter according to the situations we are facing. The most common option for dealing with this kind of situation is to not address

Finding Purpose

the dream killer, as it lessens the importance of that person. Say you're telling an aunt that you want to go for your degree in law, and your aunt tells your cousin when you're not around that you're not smart enough for that field. Yeah, it may shake up some negative feelings in your emotions, but when you take out time to address it, it gives it importance.

Now there will be times when it is necessary to confront someone who's doing things that are really affecting you, but I'll bet you can agree that the majority of the time when people are saying things about you, they actually have no direct personal effect on you. There is no need to confront them every time the dream killers are working because they can only kill our dreams if we allow them to shift our focus. Another thing we can do in these situations is to turn that negative energy into positive energy. The operative word here is energy.

Have you watched shows such as TMZ, a paparazzi program, as they stepped up to an actor with the camera in his face asking a sensitive question about his ex-wife? The paparazzi asked, "How did you lose your wife?" The actor turns to the camera, and though it is a sensitive topic, he'll say something like, "First I lost my keys, then my wallet, then I turned around, and couldn't find my wife, either."

The cameraman laughs, the actor gets a chuckle, and they even speak about how cool he is on the next day's episode. In this situation, the actor turned the negative energy into positive energy.

Here's another scenario: imagine visiting your grandmother after two years of being away, and she says, "Hi, you're fat". You have two options: you can turn around, hurt, and say, "I'm not ever visiting grandma again," or you can blame it on some other factor, like your silly cousins who usually like to instigate family drama, and laugh it off,

Finding Purpose

saying, "It's their fault." By choosing the second option, you've turned negative energy into positive energy. These are types of situations you can actually respond to but in a way that turns their attempted negativity into positivity.

Like it's been said, figuring out who's going to play on our team, and who has been playing against our team, is crucial to the success of our goals. People can both help us and hurt us, whether they are family, friends, or associates. We must identify those who will play on our team, embrace them, and do our best to keep them around.

Figure out people's positions in your life, and allow each of them to play their role. People love being a part of a team. Reflect on the feeling of connection you've felt if you've ever played a sport. Being able to support another team member gave you a sense of purpose, didn't it? And when the team you were on won the game, you probably felt a massive sense of accomplishment. That type of feeling is why people will invest their time into helping you achieve what you want to accomplish in life.

The people who are against your team may not necessarily play directly against it. As a matter of fact, like in a game, if you don't set out to challenge them, they typically don't even see you as a rival. They just may not like you. The key here is to allow people to not like you, but if you don't have to make them a rival, that's better than winning the challenge. The only reason to seek conquering an enemy is if you are attacked by the enemy. Otherwise, just keep your eyes on them, and allow their negative thoughts of you to just fade away. Never spend your valuable energy in wasted battles. You will need to use as much energy as possible as fuel toward positive actions in reaching your goals in the most successful fashion.

Prioritization Chart - People

Reflect on people that you may need, or can utilize in order to reach your goals. Prioritize them from top to bottom, #1 to #5.

The reason #1 has wider space is based on the idea that in life, we should try to provide more space for our top priorities. As we move down the list of priorities, our space should become more narrow, so it is important that we prioritize our goals based on this concept. Many times we feel that we are able to give everyone and everything equal time, but this is never the case in any single moment, or any single period of time. The way you use the priority chart can shift with time as certain circumstances change, but the fact remains that we are always giving more attention to one area than the others regarding how we seek to achieve the goals in our lives.

In this space, it would be helpful for us to think about the people that we could most utilize in helping us reach a goal. In the coming chapters, we will continue to dissect this one goal for practice, while examining how the use of this system should expand as needed.

Finding Purpose

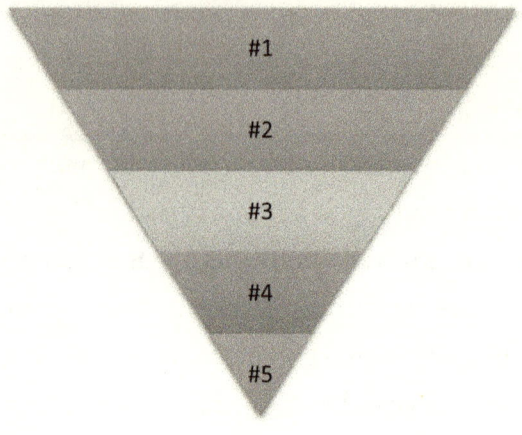

Chapter Eight

JOHN KENDRICK'S REFLECTION

What exactly is purpose?

A lot of us walk through life with a certain numbness and desperation for a deeper connection, searching for something more meaningful. The late Tupac Shakur once said, "If you can't find nothing to live for, you better find something to die for". Of all the wonderful days in our lives, two will sure stand out – the day we are born and the day we discover our purpose.

For some who are spiritually or religiously inclined, the purpose has to do with the instruction from God who gives direction to the life of every creature. Other than this, life purpose is the message you drive home with your life while on Earth. It is something that applies to us all whether we are religious or not. It does not matter your age, socio-economic status, or your background. If you desire to live a meaningful life, discovering your purpose is inevitable.

Helen Keller once said, "The only thing worse than being blind is having sight but no vision." The purpose is the starting point of a meaningful life; you know who you are and what you represent, and this gives you clarity, and also helps you put long-term goals in place. Purpose is a unique phenomenon. It is individualistic and, as such,

Finding Purpose

only you can actually figure out yours, sometimes with the help of others. It is not something you can decipher from being pressured, forced, or discovered by merely worrying about it. Here are some reasons why knowing and understanding your purpose is important.

1. Purpose gives direction and meaning. A man with a purpose will find meaning in whatever he does. This is in contrast to an individual without a purpose that just lives a random existence.

2. Once you can find your purpose, then you can begin the transition to your ideal life

3. Purpose brings about drive and passion. A man with a purpose knows where he is heading and how to get there. He also has an incredible amount of energy that keeps him on the journey. Every day presents new opportunities for such people to live extraordinary lives. The day is never a drag as you always look forward to what you do.

4. Having a purpose allows you to achieve success on your terms. Beyond being an end in itself, success should also have a natural effect on doing what you love. A man that knows his purpose will joyfully give his life to pursuing it. This is because he will derive fulfillment.

Now, with all this talk about purpose, you must realize that it does not have to be enormous as the significance of your influence has nothing to do with its scale. There are people for everything, and this is what gives balance to our world.

In our fast-paced world today, there are lots of distractions that cause people to lose focus, thus missing their purpose. These distractions can come in the form of daily activities (entertainment,

Finding Purpose

food, a chronic habit of staying busy that prevents you from reflecting on life and other habits). It can also come in the form of our preconceived expectations and ideas of what a worthy purpose is. Getting past these distractions helps you identify your purpose

The question remains, how can you identify your purpose?

For me, understanding my purpose came at an early age. I didn't really understand it at the time but realized I was very comfortable and passionate about being of service to others and this is what I have done now every day for the past 18 years, and I just happen to get paid for it monetarily.

As a child, whenever I was being of service to others, whether serving on the usher board or playing the drums for the church, or working with my uncle passing out flyers and selling candy bars. I was constantly told by others that I was really great at what I did. For me this came naturally, it wasn't something I felt uncomfortable with or had to work too hard at.

As I grew older, my passion to serve others grew as well, and I began hearing others say that I had a gift for understanding the needs of others. I remember at the age of twelve, one day, I was passing out flyers promoting my uncle's business. I would walk the neighborhood and inside one particular swap meet, I frequently visited. There was a Korean man who owned two men's clothing businesses inside, and he would see me there almost daily working. One day, he asked me my name and I told him "My name is John, John Kendrick". He replied, "My name is Young Gin Ha." We shook hands, and he begin to compliment me on being a hard worker. Little did I know, this would be the beginning of something bigger to come.

Finding Purpose

One day I was walking through the swap meet and Mr. Young Gin Ha just had an encounter with a shoplifter who walked by his store, grabbed two pairs of pants, and ran away. Little did I know this was something that repeatedly happened at the store, due to the location of the store being by the exit. After the incident, I walked over to Mr. Ha and begin talking about what happened and how often it happened. I then began talking to Mr. Ha about the need for him to hire me for the weekends and during the Christmas break, which was the busiest time, to keep an eye on things and prevent theft from occurring. Did I mention, at this time I am a short, skinny twelve-year-old kid? Anyway, he agreed.

Now, most people would have said "surprisingly, he agreed". But to me, this was no surprise, it was something that I expected to happen, and had every bit of confidence that it would. I realized that his decision to hire me didn't start on that day, it was all the other days he watched me work. The days I greeted him and stopped by to have a little small talk. It was all these little things combined that allowed him to make a decision to hire me for the next four years during my Christmas vacation. This was one of the points in my life that I look back on and realize the power in working and living in one's purpose even though, at the time, I didn't understand it.

Identifying one's purpose may not be obvious. It is something that takes time, even years for some. However, finding it no matter how long is worth it. Here are some ideas that can help you:

1. What is that thing you love doing even if you do not get paid?

    This can help you make a career/job, one that you love to do especially since it is tied directly to your purpose. Although the way you choose to earn a living may not necessarily have anything to do with your purpose, earning a living and fulfilling your purpose at the same time makes life a lot more interesting.

2. What do people say about your ability?

    As much as you should be careful to gravitate toward a path others set out, it is also good to listen to what others say about us; especially those you know are sincere. Have people told you they feel a lot better when they share their life issues with you? This could be a pointer.

3. Is there something you have a strong desire to do that will give you a deep feeling of satisfaction? Keep asking this question even if you do not have an answer yet. Also, keep an open mind and your eyes open for possible clues as the answer will certainly show up in time.

4. How do you intend to make the world a better place?

    The world we know today faces many problems. Picking a problem you know you can contribute to solving could just be what you need to bring joy, happiness, and fulfillment to your life and the lives of others. It is all about making a difference

5. How would you want to be remembered?

    Now, if you knew you would be dead a year from now, what would you like to be remembered for? What would you spend your days doing? Thinking about the fact that our time here on Earth is limited can help us re-evaluate our lives and give priority to those things that are important. People with no sense of direction or purpose usually do not know what is

Finding Purpose

important to them or what their values are. When this is the case, they end up taking and running with the values of others which usually ends in misery.

Purpose gives meaning to our lives so that every area – whether in our family, academics, and even jobs – becomes fulfilling. Without purpose, we roam through life with no direction. It is all about knowing who you are, the direction you are gravitating to, and how you might get there.

Once I realized what living a meaningful life meant to me, and I identified one purpose, it started becoming easier for me to see more.
- Catherine Frenes

Chapter Nine

STEP 5. ENJOY THE PROCESS

NOTES

> Enjoy The Process (Tools):
> *Massage the "not" out of – I do not have Endurance/Perseverance*

What tools are you utilizing to be resilient?

As indicated by this book's title, *Finding Purpose*, we've been exploring the prospect of building effective relationships, as well as the process of self-care as we identify our strengths and weaknesses. In saying this, there is another important aspect to finding and living in our purpose. Whenever you are attempting to accomplish something in life, whether it is a small task or a large goal, both people and things are components that need to be utilized.

I purposely did not employ the word 'use', because I did not want it to be misconstrued in this context. A more appropriate term to rely on would be 'utilize', as the difference between 'use' and 'utilize' is that when you 'use' someone you are likely disregarding how they feel and being unappreciative of their contribution. When you 'utilize' someone, you are appreciating what they are contributing to your

Finding Purpose

efforts and you are also staying in tune with how they feel about the contribution. When you utilize someone, they feel good about not only contributing but also being a part of what you are working to accomplish. When you allow someone to feel like they are a part of the goal, you will see a higher level of commitment from them due to the feeling that they are more invested in the effort.

As we speak about utilizing people as tools, we also have to speak about utilizing materials and resources. Those resources can include formal and informal education, plus they can include financial, methods of transportation, whether it's a car or an airplane. They can also include very specific tools for the industry or trade that you are working within.

Oftentimes when I am speaking to someone about what they're trying to accomplish, it seems as if they have not organized the tools that they will need to accomplish that goal. Or it may seem as if they have not yet gathered the tools that will be required for their task. Sometimes we have to ask ourselves what is realistic to expect from what we are pursuing, and whether we can accomplish something in terms of our tools' effectiveness and accessibility.

I'm not saying that we shouldn't shoot for the stars because we should, but what I am saying is that we need a set a realistic plan in place that can bring our dreams to fruition. In fact, I personally believe that we should set goals for ourselves that are so high that most people believe the goal itself is unrealistic. But at the same time, I am of the belief that the plan that we have in place to reach that goal should be very realistic.

Personally, I've had many goals in life before I was able to narrow down what was my ultimate passion. One thing about me is that even

Finding Purpose

at a very early age, I knew that having the right tools was important in order to accomplish my goals in life.

For instance, when I played football in high school, I knew that I needed football cleats, a helmet, and shoulder pads. I needed pads on my body, along with any other additional accessories, to protect myself. Later, when I ran track, I knew that I needed spikes, as well as a jogging suit to keep my body warm in between races. Then in my early twenties, I decided to go to barbering school. While I was in class, my instructor said you need tools and you need to take care of your tools.

He said the way you wrap your wires around your electric clippers, the way you clean your supplies, and the way you organize your supplies should all be done with care. He showed us how our tools were directly connected to our financial success, and that we should put even more care than what would be accepted as normal into our tools.

When I was working in the entertainment industry and writing music, I knew that I needed music equipment to be accessible to me. Following this revelation, I went out after saving money and purchased a small home studio. Even though I had opportunities to use other people's equipment, I wanted to have equipment that was the most accessible to my own specific workflow. I wanted to make sure that if I had an idea or wanted to take action at any moment in my music career, my tools would be immediately accessible to me to do so.

For instance, if someone asked me to write a song for them, I did not want to respond by saying "let me see if I can borrow someone's keyboard." When I bought my equipment, it was because I wanted to be able to meet deadlines, to work within timelines, and, generally

Finding Purpose

speaking, to be able to deliver a product quickly that would fit the needs of my client.

During certain difficult financial times, I would sometimes want to give up and sell my equipment. There have been other times when I've worked in other industries where I was tempted to sell my tools in order to accomplish my goal. I've had to make decisions about whether I would eat Top Ramen noodles on a daily basis or sell my microphone for a steak dinner. There have been times when I've had to make a decision about selling a pair of electric hair clippers just so I could eat my favorite hamburger off the sands on Hermosa Beach. And there was a moment when I was even beginning to post my tools on the internet to be sold. Once I had a few of my items posted, a friend of mine saw it and contacted me, saying "Steve, take those things off of the internet immediately."

He said, "You never want to sell your tools in order to make ends meet." He said that if you are struggling with money, then that is a sign that you need to strategize better on how to increase your tools. He said that you may need to become more creative in the way that you approach your work. He said that you may need to build a stronger network. Then he said, "The one thing you don't want to do is get into the cycle of trying to sell and rebuy your equipment because inevitably you will get to the point that you can no longer afford to buy it back."

His comments really opened my eyes to the importance of tools, and it had me question what I would actually do if I did not have the tools I'd need to accomplish my goals? The fact is, we need tools and we need people. When we are attempting to live in our purpose, we need to make sure that we have the tools that will help us maintain longevity in order to keep our careers on track. That said, these

Finding Purpose

sentiments do bring to mind the importance of assessing the actual quality of the tools that we find ourselves using.

I understand that there are times when we may consider using just the bare minimum in materials to get your jobs done. But if you really think about things that you have successfully accomplished in the past, you can probably think of how your task demanded a high quality tool to get the result that you wanted. Those tools may have included anything, such as a chair designed to support your back for four to eight hours a day, or a special pen that will relax your hand as you write. When it comes to picking tools that can help you complete tasks in your business or for particular jobs, you'd likely want them to be advanced in quality.

Sometimes it can be easy to ponder how cheaply you can accomplish a goal by not using the ideal tool for the job, but a lower quality variation of what would normally be prescribed. I'm saying this because many times when we think about the tools we need to help us fulfill our life's purpose, we, unfortunately, cut ourselves short.

Maybe the tool that you would need could involve a workshop that may cost $300 or 400 for a weekend retreat. Maybe it could be a book that is priced between 30 and $40. Maybe that tool could be the cost of college tuition or a car for $50,000. It isn't that we want to spend as much money on our tools as possible, but we do want to make sure that look at the value that we're getting for our money. Sometimes it is more important to when a tool that is expensive in price is necessary to have than to settle for a tool that won't be nearly as effective in the results that it will help bring about.

Ask yourself, "what is it worth for me to have the equipment that I need in order to accomplish my personal goals?" "What is it worth for me to have the equipment that will help me fulfill my life's purpose?" When we enter a stage of life and begin to reflect back on what we've accomplished to get to that point, many times we will end up placing less value on the amount of money we spent or made and more on the value of our contributions to the lives of others.

Prioritization Chart – Tools

Take a moment to think about the tools that you may need to accomplish a goal that you would have in mind. Remember, you have more space for the #1 priority than #5. For instance, to become a barber, a top priority may be education and training, followed by such priorities as hair clippers, scissors, and whatever else they may be. You may need to achieve all of your priorities to achieve the success that you want, but which one would you need to satisfy first? What is the most important to you right now, at this moment?

Reminder, we are mainly dissecting the top goal slot that was previously mentioned within the prior chapter.

Finding Purpose

Tools

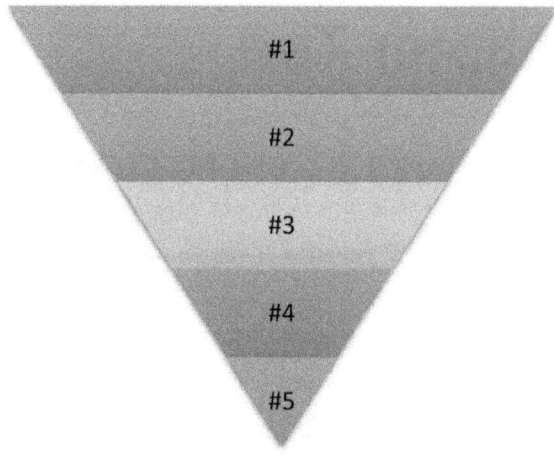

Chapter Ten

CATHERINE FRENES'S REFLECTION

I can easily recall the time in my life when I started asking myself the question, "What's my purpose in life;" it wasn't that long ago. I know many people have asked themselves this very same question and if you never have, you will or you're one of the few lucky people who have always known. To find the answer, I knew I must look deep within myself.

Self-reflection, it's me, it's the person I hear in my head all day, all night, so why does getting in touch with our "inner self" seem like a mission impossible? At least it does when you've asked yourself the question, "What's my purpose in life," and you do not yet have the answer.

So what does having purpose mean anyway, right? I knew I had to answer this question on my own to ever answer the question "What's my purpose in life?" Searching to answer this, I learned a lot about myself and what is important to me.

I came to a conclusion of what living in purpose means. I feel that having a purpose is to live with meaning, know and feel confident about your values and beliefs, believe in who you are and what you want to represent, and stand for in life. I was raised by a single mother

Finding Purpose

who put all of her trust and faith in Jesus, and I witnessed miracles. I took my mother's same values in Christianity and use my belief in those values as my life guide. I trust that if I live my life following my belief then the road I'm on today is where I am meant to be and will take me to where I am meant to go. But believing this still did not make me certain of my purpose, it opened up more questions.

Like, live with meaning...what does this even mean? Does it mean, what do I want out of life? Most people can answer this question very quickly, which makes me wonder why it's difficult for me and a lot of us to know our purpose. I knew before I was ever married that I wanted a happy marriage, a house I could make a home, a prosperous career, one day children and to somehow make a difference in the world, even if it's small and goes unnoticed. When I am retired, I want to foster dogs that need medical assistance while their forever home is found and use my free time volunteering at local charities for homeless and abused children. But where is my purpose in all of my wants? And how do all of my wants bring meaning to my life?

I have a wonderful life. I'm blessed to have more than fifty percent of my wants accomplished and yet I could only find my generic purposes. I knew my true purpose was still unknown because I had the feeling inside of me that there is something greater, I felt I was missing something. I realized I lost the passion that originally got me the things I want in life. I allowed myself to get in the rut of routine. I'm not saying routine is negative. We make it negative when we never step out of the boundaries we have set for ourselves. My life was at a standstill because of me, but life kept happening all around me.

When we are children, they say we tend to do things we are most passionate about. So in my journey to find or understand my purpose,

Finding Purpose

I began doing things I enjoyed as a child: dancing, roller skating, hiking, oil painting, reading, organizing anything and everything; I'm even known to be a clean freak. Then one night I was writing in my journal. I have kept one ever since my mother passed away more than a decade ago now. Anyhow, I write to document important moments, silly memories, things I don't want age to possibly take from me. So one day I may share with others all of my life experiences. It was during this moment in silence and writing I realized I don't have a purpose, but purposes!

Earlier I mentioned "generic purposes." I have learned in my journey, there is no such thing as a "generic purpose." Everything we choose to do in a day has purpose behind it or at least it should. For instance, my husband and I operate a business together. We each have certain responsibilities we handle and tasks we'll delegate, but we are working as a team to accomplish one goal. That goal we want to accomplish gives meaning to my responsibilities which fills me with purpose. We strive every day to reach our goal on purpose because doing what we love also provides the income we need.

I understand that not everyone can say they are doing what they love for income, so how is my job my purpose? Unless you really hate what you're doing, maybe you're looking at it all wrong. Because you are making income, you look at what you are doing as a job, but what drew you to your position in the first place? If you can remember that, you've located a purpose to the many I believe we have in life.

As you ask this question, you may think of how your presence has changed the life of a co-worker or you may realize something has changed in your life or you stay in your position because it's comfortable. I've learned to get out of my comfort zone and take a

Finding Purpose

chance on what really makes me happy, do what captivates me. You may even think of family and how you feel the need to be their support system. Finding purpose is a true soul-searching mission; you must seek with an open heart and mind.

I also realized in that moment of silence and writing that being a wife is very meaningful and there is nothing generic about it! Being a wife is more than just cooking dinners and doing laundry. I have a wonderful husband that God gifted me to so he will have companionship, to help him reach his full potential, to help him accomplish his purpose and be successful. I am my husband's support, I help pick him up when he is down and vice versa. We share all of life's bad times and all of life's good times. Loving my husband with all of my heart, striving every day for our lives to be better together is one of my life's greatest purposes. One day we hope to have children together, we've even thought about adopting children and that will bring even more purpose to my life as the Bible states one purpose of marriage is to create a stable home in which children can grow and thrive.

My husband and I got married on our 10 year Anniversary of being a couple and have been married for four years now. When it occurred to me, I was crazy to have thought that being a wife was a generic purpose, my marriage started to blossom all over again. I'm able to enjoy all the little things that come with being a wife, and I am grateful I have a purpose in my husband and his dreams.

I believe my upbringing to be a Christian has helped me in my journey of finding my purpose. According to the Bible, our purpose, the reason we are here, is for God's glory. In other words, our purpose is to praise God, worship him, proclaim his greatness, and accomplish his will. I do my very best to help others in need and spread the love

Finding Purpose

and word of God. I'm human and make mistakes, but I treat each new day, just as it is, a new day, and strive to be the person God intends for me to be.

I know my faith in the Lord has allowed me to see how to set my limitations in life to accept that with God all things are possible. We have to believe in ourselves and know we are capable of a lot more than most of us give ourselves credit for; in fact, I am probably my own worst critic.

We should not pass judgment on ourselves, and we should not pass judgment on others, it cripples our ability to live to our fullest potential. As previously mentioned, I believe we make our own limitations in life and I feel we should push our limits to the point where we make our palms sweat and always reach for the stars in order to live our fullest. We must live using all of our potentials and following our hearts, using our values, beliefs, and morals as our guide to living a life that is meaningful.

Once I realized what living a meaningful life meant to me, and I identified one purpose, it started becoming easier for me to see more. Proverbs 16:9 states "The heart of man plans his way, but the Lord establishes his steps." So I re-defined my goals, sat with my husband, and redefined our goals, our life plan. I felt back on track, I felt confident in my life plan and my life started changing. I no longer felt I was living in the rut of routine, or just going thru life's motions, but I felt excited. I'm excited to fulfill my life goals and to keep dreaming of new life adventures. I feel confident in the goals my husband and I have set for our lives together, and I feel confident in the goals I have set for myself. Making goals and holding myself accountable to accomplish them truly gives me a sense of purpose. I've learned purpose can only

Finding Purpose

be found in doing, and the more you do, the more life surprises you and you surprise yourself, at least I have.

When my eyes opened to all the possibilities life has in store for me, everything in my life began changing. I no longer felt that our restaurant was just a job to pay the bills. I saw the potential it was giving me to make a difference in people's lives, in my own life. Every day I am blessed with the opportunity to meet new people and have a chance to leave a lasting impression on them. Maybe they were having a bad day and I was able to bring a smile to their faces or maybe they did the same for me.

During my personal journey to learn to live with purpose, I really feel like I have more than one. Don't limit yourself to thinking there is only one thing on this earth you are meant to do or find that one thing that you think defines you and then stop searching; always be open to possibilities.

As silly as it may sound, I even found my purpose in being a dog owner. I have found meaning in nurturing, loving, and providing them with a safe home. In return, dogs bring me motivation. Dogs do not understand sympathy for themselves, therefore no matter their mood, they will also show unconditional love and loyalty and working dogs will always get their job done. Dogs remind me to have patience, be loyal to my beliefs, stay in faith, and show compassion and empathy toward others no matter my mood. "Treat others the way you wish to be treated." This is my rule of thumb.

Are you having trouble defining your purposes in life? Give yourself a good long look in the mirror, reconnect with your inner You. Ask yourself what you love, what makes you happy? What do you enjoy? When was the last time you did something for yourself? When

Finding Purpose

was the last time you did something for someone else? When we listen at the heart level, we will always be guided forward in a way that serves us. The degree to which we listen to and act on our callings determines how fulfilled we will be with our lives.

So do something out of your norm, get out of your rut of routine and try something new. Listen to your inner voice. I truly believe you will discover your purpose or purposes like I have when you discover what you enjoy and start living life to the fullest.

I always remind myself to be open to new possibilities because I never know when I will discover a new purpose life has for me. Remember, we all have a reason for our existence. We may not always identify our own calling, but we may very well have touched the hearts of others and, as Christians, that is better than anything else we can do for ourselves!

When you have to do things, you are not in a place of love. When you do it because you want, you are doing it in a place of love. I put myself in those situations as much as I can. If I have to do something, I let it go. Quickly. – Adriana Soto

---

Chapter Eleven

STEP 6. RUNNING ON FIRE

NOTES

Running on Fire (Take Action):
Massage the "not" out of - I will not win

Reflect on your progress

So here is the final section regarding people, tools, and action. One of the most difficult parts of fulfilling a purpose is actually putting your actions into practice. It is true that in some cases, I have found people expressing why it is difficult to put action into place is because they're looking for perfection in their plan, or they are seeking validation. While this can many times be the case, typically speaking, the purpose that we pursue is usually connected to the vision of our lives that is given directly to us.

We cannot expect others to see the vision that has been cast for our lives in the same ways that we can. Each of us is an individual and each of us receives our visions in our own special ways. Waiting for someone to validate our actions toward our purpose is like waiting for someone else to receive the vision that we have for ourselves, which doesn't make a lot of sense at all.

Sometimes you can be moved to question whether you're qualified enough to accomplish your goal. This happens often, particularly when people are led to question their own credentials or the influence they have on others before deciding to take a specific action.

Be under no illusion - you are your credentials. Your credentials include your personal life experiences, both informal and formal, and anything else that has contributed to the decisions that inform your methods for taking action. The nature of your credentials can fall under many categories, such as spiritual, scientific, psychological, or social. But whatever your credentials may be, it is not always your responsibility to explain to others why or how you are qualified to fulfill your purpose.

If there is a legitimate position that requires a certain level of expertise, it's up to you to obtain-that specific expertise. It is up to you to acquire those specific credentials in order to operate in those positions and be able to vouch for possessing them when seeking to be hired by the organization in question. But, generally speaking, if your purpose is to, for example, feed the homeless, or create an organization that promotes clean energy, or helps people who have experienced abuse to believe in themselves, then there are usually no specific qualifications required in order for you to begin operating within that space. This is normally because these kinds of tasks are immensely important in the scope of society, but are usually conducted in a way that is less formal than the average corporate or industrial occupations that you would be required to interview for.

Finding Purpose

So, I have a question for you: are you currently taking action within your purpose? Are you currently operating within that purpose? If not, what is your reason? Is there something stopping you from moving forward and taking steps of action toward that reaching that place?

A few years ago, this was a dilemma that I faced personally. I had made a decision to write my first book. When I made that decision, I was at a time in my career when I was still attending workshops and teaching life skills to two people who were having a horrible time dealing with challenges in their lives. Many of these challenges were preventing them from moving forward within their educational pursuits and in their careers. My job was to help them understand their full potential so that they could move forward towards their successful destinies with confidence and skill.

After conducting various workshops within several demographic groups, such as young college students in law enforcement, I felt that it would be highly effective to compile the workshop material that I was studying into a book that could be made available to people around the world.

As I began writing this book and informing people about the process, they started asking this very question: "Steve, what qualifies you to write this content?" I had already earned the position to practice the material that I was writing about, and I had already seen the outcomes of people who applied the knowledge that I would be examining. I wasn't famous, but each individual that I worked with who applied the material that I taught saw some type of enhancement within their lives. I received many thank you letters, emails, phone calls

Finding Purpose

from people who wanted to express the positivity they had experienced from being advised and tutored by me.

So, as time moved on and I began getting closer to reaching the end of my book writing process, people continued to ask me: "Steve, what are your qualifications, and what are your credentials?" Once I decided to answer them, I told them that my credentials were all the outcomes being expressed by the people who said that their lives had been enhanced by what I had contributed to them.

When you respond to people who question why or how you are qualified for a job, that response doesn't have to be arrogant, but the response should be confident. You know your value as an individual or a unique person; you have something to offer the world that no one else can offer. You are your biggest asset because when you were created, it was with unique attributes that are unlike anyone else around you. Only you can offer the world the gifts that you have been blessed with. And you giving to the world from the gifts and talents that you already possess edifies the lives that we touch, whether it is spiritually, psychologically, socially, physically, economically, or emotionally.

It is my experience that when you lift up those around you, there is no reason to seek a reward because the reward will find you. You know that you are following this rule of life effectively when it becomes evident that you are living within your purpose.

Prioritization Chart – Action

Here you will lay out action steps. What would be not the only most important, but most realistic and achievable action step to attempt, right now? What can you do today to begin working towards this goal?

Finding Purpose

Reminder, we are only dissecting the top goal that was previously mentioned within the prior chapters.

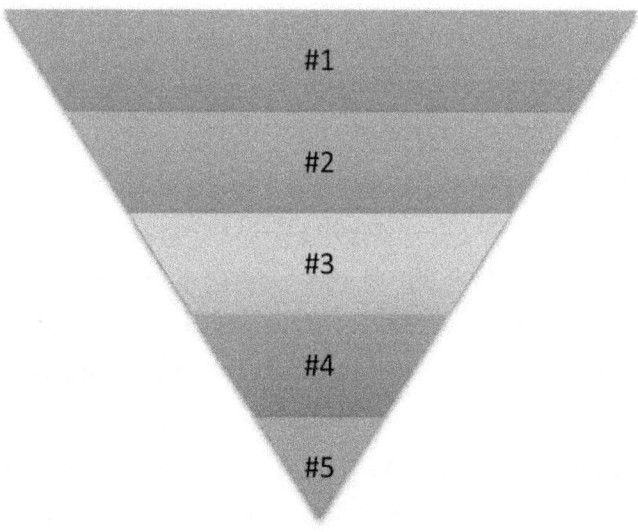

Chapter Twelve

Adriana Soto's Reflection

Basically I realized my own purpose when I found myself stuck and not knowing what I should be doing or what I'm here for. There could be a point in life where you don't know what you are doing or what you are put into this world for. When I started doing inter-search I remembered what a mentor told me, "be still and be it." Over time, I realized what that quote meant. It means to be with yourself, and without distractions.

The world distracts us from our creator and ourselves. Even with just you and God, our Creator, you are all of who you need to be. Get in touch with the vibration of our Creator and reach who you are destined to fully become. Start to realize what you love, because Our purpose is within what we love the most. Then pursue it like a mission.

When you love what you do, without expecting anything in return, you are likely within your purpose. For each of us, our purpose is different. One quote that I like is "the secret to living is giving." I have realized through the years that when you give, and it comes from love, love is one of the most powerful vibrations that you can experience. With love, you can interrupt any other vibration. With love, you can break through barriers.

Finding Purpose

How do you find purpose? Your first act from a place of love in order to see what it brings. With everything that comes, remember, the ultimate purpose is to love, and unconditionally. Through the process, know that everything we experience is a lesson. We learn through these experiences. At times, we may need to be vulnerable, though it may hurt, because, through vulnerability, we allow ourselves to receive those experiences. We usually protect ourselves from it. This is one of the ways that life tries to distract us from finding our purpose. In other ways, technology, invented by man, could also be a tool to distract us, as it often prevents us from being still, being present with who we are.

Our past is one of the biggest barriers that we encounter. Our past experiences can stop us from fulfilling what we should. If something we truly loved caused us pain, we may avoid trying it again. We as humans are driven by pain and pleasure. We run from one and run towards the other. But when we realize that every situation that we find ourselves in is for a reason, whether it is good or bad, it drives us closer to our purpose, while meaning was pulled from that situation for our good. Be mindful, that sometimes the wrong decisions could take us to the wrong places.

When you are being forced to do things, you are not operating in a place of love. When you do it because you desire, you are doing it in a place of love. I put myself in desired situations as much as I can. If I feel forced to do something, I let it go. Quickly.

My purpose is to help others to see the light through my own experiences.

PART 2

Finding Purpose

Sometimes, when we allow our past to dictate what we do, we end up in places and with people that we don't even want to be with. When we don't have role models growing up we may search for role models to fulfill that role.

In my own experience, I made many wrong choices. Due to those wrong choices, I ended up facing circumstances that completely changed my life.

I was looking for safety and to feel a part of something and to have control in every aspect of my life. It was a self-destructive environment and selfish.

This led to a point that set a desire for change deep inside me, but I did not know how to change.

I went to school and attended classes. That's where I learned about personal development. Then I became a facilitator and started talking to the girls about what I discovered about life. That's when I knew my purpose was to talk to people and help them see what I finally saw. No matter where you come from, no matter what your path is, you can always recreate yourself and do what you want to do in life. Once I left, I was determined to become the best version of myself I could be.

I worked three jobs, read books, and attended seminars. I cut things and people out of my life, including family. It was my daughter and me. I had to move away from my old neighborhood as I learned that the love I have for my daughter was bigger than the love I had on the streets.

During this process, I had a mentor that I would talk to on a daily basis. And now, I have a few mentors, because I have not stopped working on myself.

Finding Purpose

Through life experiences, I learned that the only way you can help someone is to first love them unconditionally. You don't expect anything in return, not for money, not for love. Even if they are an addict, it does not matter. It can only happen through unconditional love.

Chapter Thirteen

STEP 7. CELEBRATING THE VICTORY

NOTES

Celebrating the Victory

Reflection – Meditation – Balance - Serenity

In this chapter of *Finding Purpose*, we will discuss the celebration of victory. It can be highly motivational to celebrate the victory in either finding our ultimate purpose, finding a general purpose, or having a better idea of how to search for our purpose. Finding purpose is not always an easy task. For some people, it may come naturally, and for others, it may take conscious effort. For some people, it may take months, and for others, it may even take years.

Still, we all find some degree of purpose in our lives at different stages. You may find an adolescent who is living deep within their purpose and has already been able to accomplish creating an application for computers. On the other hand, you may have someone living in their 40s, who is completely confused about what their purpose is in their life.

Finding Purpose

I'm a strong believer that we all have a purpose in life, and I'm also a believer that our purpose is revealed during different stages in our lives. However, we must be conscious of when purpose is revealed to us so that we can take advantage of the opportunity to live within it. While we are living in our purpose it is also important for us to reflect on those positive experiences and the positive impacts that we may have had on someone else's life.

It is important that we take time to meditate in order to connect with deeper parts of ourselves and clear our minds of the everyday stresses that can keep us occupied. We must apply serenity and balance to our lives so that we don't become overwhelmed with the consumption of responsibilities that can seem to never end. You are worthy to celebrate your victories that are related to your purpose, so we must massage that "not" out of the highly toxic phrase "I am not worthy" that may be lingering somewhere in our subconscious.

What does celebrating a victory look like to you? When you are celebrating, are you expecting to receive a tangible award, such as a plaque or trophy? If so, there is nothing wrong with you creating that plaque or trophy for yourself. You can even create a certificate, print it out, and sign it, all with the purpose of acknowledging yourself. Monumentalizing a moment requires no necessary authorization from someone else on the outside. You can validate your own accomplishments and be proud the same way that other people can.

Alternatively, celebrating your victory may be as simple as going out and buying ice cream for yourself. Celebrating your victory may be treating yourself to a new pair of shoes or a new outfit. Maybe celebrating your victory could be signing up for a mixed martial arts class that you've always wanted to try. During this chapter, I want you

Finding Purpose

to really think about what a celebration signifies to you and what some of the things are that you can do to celebrate those moments of purpose-related accomplishment, whether big or small. You could have set a goal to feed 10 homeless people in the period of a month, and ended up meeting that goal. By the same token, you may have set your mind to create a good renowned movie and stand on the stage of the Academy Awards in conjunction with that film in order to bring awareness to an important issue. In either case, you should celebrate that accomplishment that is directly related to your purpose.

It doesn't matter how big or small, it is extremely important to take a pause every now and then to remind ourselves of what we have contributed to society. We should do this for a couple of reasons. One reason is to acknowledge what we have accomplished, and how it is related to our purpose. The other reason is to narrow down what we have not accomplished, and begin strategizing and meditating on what we need to do to fulfill these gaps and create a more purposeful life.

Purpose gives meaning and value to us as well as those around us in the world that live in. This is why I say, regardless of how luxurious your car may be, how large your house is, the value of your Jewelry, the status of your career, or the level of your education, life's greatest accomplishment is finding purpose.

As mentioned before, this system expands as needed up to 5 goals, and seems to keep realistic track of your progress. We will begin by breaking down goal number 1, then repeat the same steps as we move on to goal #2, to #3, etc. Feel free to draw this graph on paper, if you would like to avoid writing in the book, or you can also use a pencil.

Finding Purpose

Begin listing 5 goals –

PTA GOALS

P

T

Goal 01

Goal 02

Goal 03

Goal 04

Goal 05

A

Place Goal #1
in the Middle Triangle –

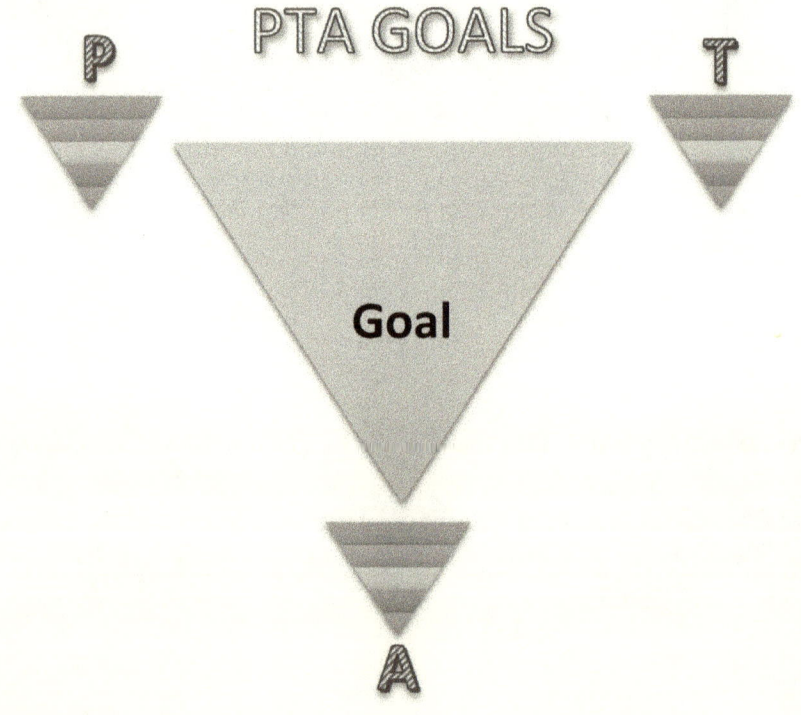

Starting with P, list all of the people needed or who could be utilized in order to accomplish a goal #1.

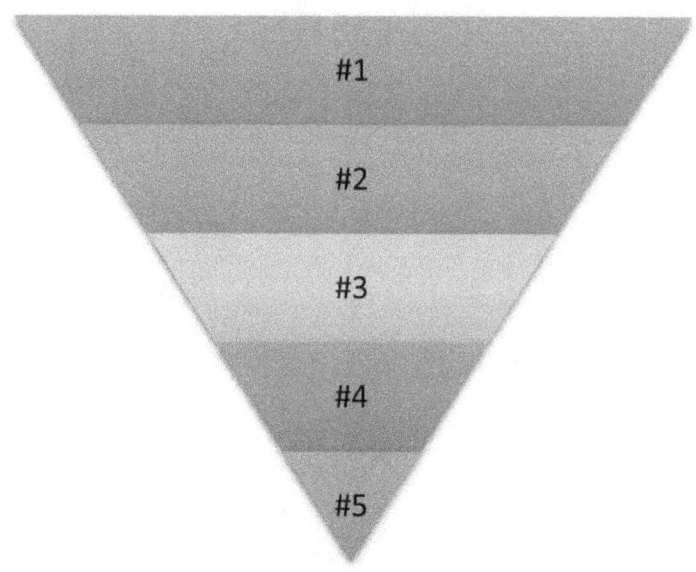

Now moving to T, list all of the Tools needed or that could just be utilized in order to accomplish Goal #1. (Education, equipment, financial resources, etc.)

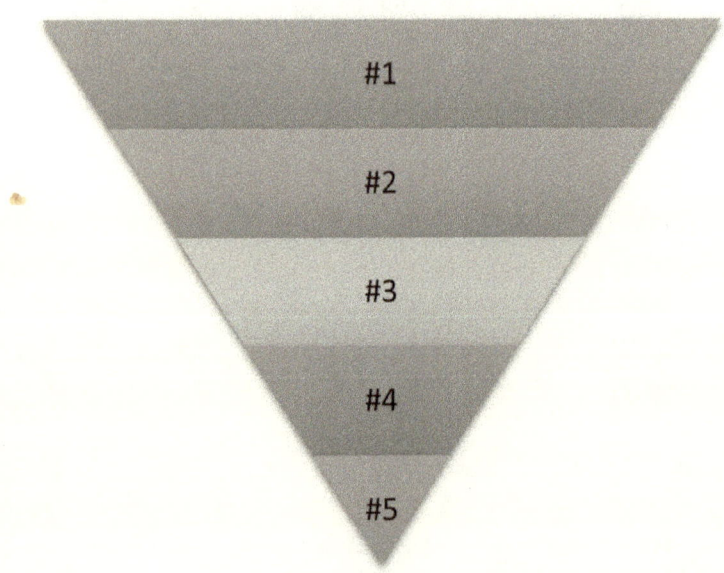

Lastly with A, list the realistic action steps that you can take right now or in the near future, in order to accomplish Goal #1.

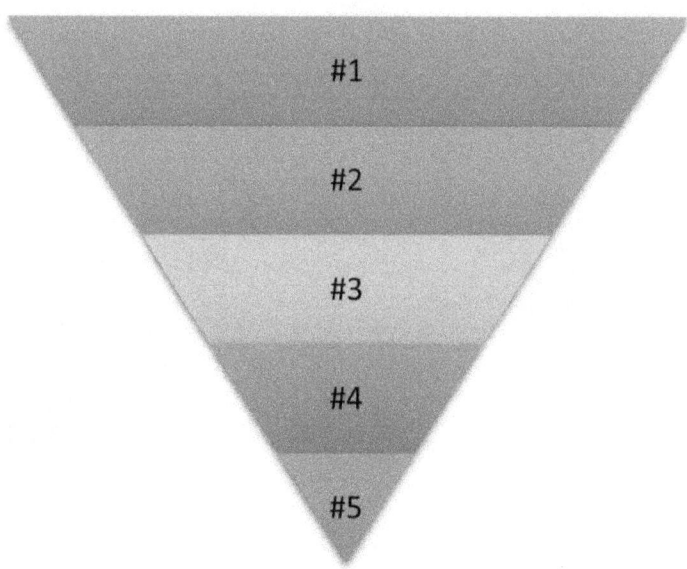

PURPOSE BLUEPRINT WORKBOOK

Finding Purpose

PURPOSE IN ACTION

Creating a roadmap with purpose

Dream to Reality Portfolio

① **Develop the details** - Branding who you are (purpose, who it involves)

② **Necessities to Accomplish your goal** - Leverage your Heart and Mind. (tools, people)

③ **Ways to Acquire the Tools** - Save Time and money by proper talent placement. (financial)

④ **Educational Requirements** (special training)

⑤ **Approach After Education** - Become a master storyteller, (getting a foot in the door, appearance) elevator sells pitch

⑥ **Time Line of Accomplishments** - Building products. (Long and Short term goals, action steps)

⑦ **Your Fan Base** - Build Trust and Rapport with your peers, audience and/or Customers. (Data Base)

⑧ **Push abroad** (what it takes - Perseverance, Endurance, Patience)

⑨ **Staying Alive** (how will you maintain your accomplishments) your product may be old to you, but it's new to the world.

⑩ **Enjoy the Benefits Reached** (responsibility, giving back gives back)

Finding Purpose

Generally, our passions are wrapped around or within our Purpose. Commonly, people are able to easily identify things they are passionate about, though they may find it more challenging to identify their purpose. This purpose can be within a job, family, spiritual walk, or generally in life. As we build our goals, we will begin to identify what is within our passions and goals, that leads us to identifying and walking within our purpose.

Describe what you are passionate about:

Family:

Career:

Life: (spirituality, health, etc.)

Finding Purpose

Describe what you feel responsible for within the following:

Family:

Career:

Life: (spirituality, health, etc.)

PORTFOLIO

Participants will create a portfolio, with highlights of their steps towards finding and living in purpose.

Dream in detail

(Purpose, who it involves)
Who am I/Born Identity
Mission, Goal, Purpose

Purpose is the thing that you feel you were made to do and were put here on the Earth to accomplish. It's the thing that you would gladly do for free, but realize that you could profit greatly if you can make it as your full-time profession. It's the thing that no matter how far you may stray away, you always find yourself coming right back to it and making it the central focus of your life. It's the talent that you seem to have always had a knack for, even when you were a kid. It's also the thing that seems so hard for everyone else to accomplish but seems to come extremely easy to you.

In essence, your purpose is likely linked directly with whatever you are exceptionally talented in that also happens to come very easy to you, especially when compared to other people that you come across throughout your life's adventures.

Dream: What would you consider to be a life's dream?

Finding Purpose

Mission: Create a mission statement for your life –

Career

How do you envision your career within the next 1 to 5 years?

Family

How do you envision your family within the next 1 to 5 years?

Finding Purpose

Life (spirituality, health, etc.)

How do you envision your life within the next 1 to 5 years?

```
┌─────────────────────────────────────────┐
│                                         │
│                                         │
│                                         │
└─────────────────────────────────────────┘
```

Purpose: Are there any common themes within how you envision your future?

```
┌─────────────────────────────────────────┐
│                                         │
│                                         │
│                                         │
└─────────────────────────────────────────┘
```

Do your goals involve working with anyone? (Who and why)

Finding Purpose

What's Needed to Turn a Dream

(Tools, Description)
Direction/Overcoming Obstacles

As we speak about utilizing tools, we are speaking about utilizing people, materials and resources. Those resources can include formal and informal education, plus they can include financial, methods of transportation, whether it's a car or an airplane. They can also include very specific tools for the industry or trade that you are working within.

Oftentimes when I am speaking to someone about what they're trying to accomplish, it seems as if they have not organized the tools that they will need to accomplish that goal. Or it may seem as if they have not yet gathered the tools that will be required for their task. Sometimes we have to ask ourselves what is realistic to expect from what we are pursuing, and whether we can accomplish something in terms of our tools' effectiveness and accessibility.

What tools might you need to acquire in order to fulfill what you envision?

Family: Gear, equipment, education, finances

1.
2.
3.
4.
5.
6.
7.
8.
9.

Career: Gear, equipment, education, finances

1.
2.
3.
4.
5.
6.
7.
8.
9.

Finding Purpose

Life: Gear, equipment, education, finances

1.
2.
3.
4.
5.
6.
7.
8.
9.

Finding Purpose

Prioritization Chart – Tools

Take a moment to think about the tools that you may need, to accomplish a goal that you have in mind. Remember, you have more space for the #1 priority than #5.

For instance, to become a barber, a top priority may be education and training, followed by such priorities as hair clippers, scissors, and whatever else they may be. You may need to achieve all of your priorities to achieve the success that you want, but which one would you need to satisfy first?

What is the most important tool for you right now, at this moment?

For each individual goal, you will prioritize the tools you will need to utilize to accomplish it, #1 being top priority, moving down.

Exercise - Thinking about how you envision your family, career and life over the next 1 to 5 years listed above, document a number next to the tools you might need, from priority #1 to #5.

Finding Purpose

Tools

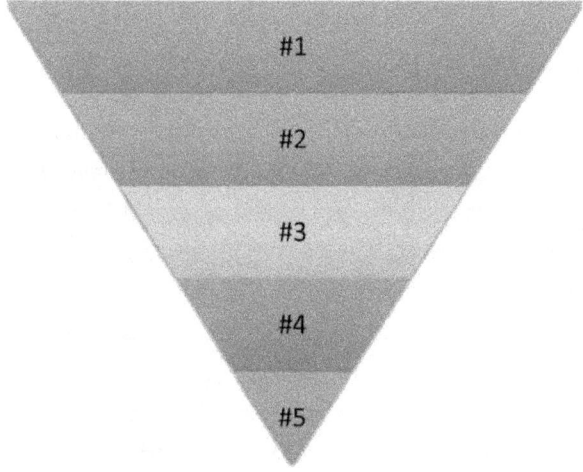

Ways to Acquire the Tools

(Financial, etc)

How will we financially support building our Purpose?

I understand that there are times when we may consider using just the bare minimum in materials to get your jobs done. But if you really think about things that you have successfully accomplished in the past, you can probably think of how your task demanded a high quality tool to get the result that you wanted. Those tools may have included anything, such as a chair designed to support your back for four to eight hours a day, or a special pen that will relax your hand as you write. When it comes to picking tools that can help you complete tasks in your business or for particular jobs, you'd likely want them to be advanced in quality.

Sometimes it can be easy to ponder how cheaply you can accomplish a goal by not using the ideal tool for the job, but a lower quality variation of what would normally be prescribed. I'm saying this because many times when we think about the tools we need to help us fulfill our life's purpose, we, unfortunately, cut ourselves short.

Maybe the tool that you would need could involve a workshop that may cost $300 or 400 for a weekend retreat. Maybe it could be a book that is priced between 30 and $40. Maybe that tool could be the cost of college tuition or a car for $50,000. It isn't that we want to spend as much money on our tools as possible, but we do want to make sure that look at the value that we're getting for our money. Sometimes it is more important to when a tool that is expensive in price is necessary to have than to settle for a tool that won't be nearly as effective in the results that it will help bring about.

Ask yourself, "what is it worth for me to have the equipment that I need in order to accomplish my personal goals?" "What is it worth for me to have the equipment that will help me fulfill my life's purpose?" When we enter a stage of life and begin to reflect back on what we've accomplished to get to that point, many times we will end up placing less value on the amount of

Finding Purpose

money we spent or made and more on the value of our contributions to the lives of others.

Finding Purpose

Financial/Equipment sources: Circle the financial resources you have or will build:

1. Savings Account
2. Checking Account
3. CD
4. Mutual Fund
5. Grants
6. Stock
7. Bonds
8. Credit
9. Job
10. Business
11. Other

Family: Other resources

Career: Other resources

Life: Other resources

Finding Purpose

[ ]

Who holds available funding/equipment?

1. Banks
2. Credit Unions
3. Private Corporations
4. Schools
5. Hospitals
6. Courts
7. Family
8. Friends
9. Associates
10. Government

What could be your financial source(s)?

[ ]

Accessing funding: complete at least 1 of the following tasks

1. Create a 1-page Beg Letter
2. Make phone calls
3. Write grant proposals
4. Schedule an In-person conversation
5. other

Remember: resources include places for money and equipment.

Finding Purpose

Write how you will acquire resources/funds: (how much would it cost)

Finding Purpose

EDUCATION

(Training, College, Trades, Seminars, etc.)
Foundation

What type of education is needed to accomplish your dream?

- **Educational Facilities**
- **Level of education needed**
- **Amount of time to acquire education**
- **Requirements to access education**
- other

Describe training obtained:

Describe the type of training needed:

Finding Purpose

Name of training:

Name of Facility:

Location:

Finding Purpose

APPROACH AFTER EDUCATION

(Getting a foot in the door)

Prioritization Chart - People

Reflect on people that you may need, or can utilize in order to reach your goals. Prioritize them from top to bottom, #1 to #5.

The reason #1 has wider space is based on the idea that in life, we should try to provide more space for our top priorities. As we move down the list of priorities, our space should become more narrow, so it is important that we prioritize our goals based on this concept. Many times we feel that we are able to give everyone and everything equal time, but this is never the case in any single moment, or any single period of time. The way you use the priority chart can shift with time as certain circumstances change, but the fact remains that we are always giving more attention to one area than the others regarding how we seek to achieve the goals in our lives.

In this space, it would be helpful for us to think about the people that we could most utilize in helping us reach a goals.

List the people you can access right now who can help get your foot in the door. (how will you access them?)

Finding Purpose

People

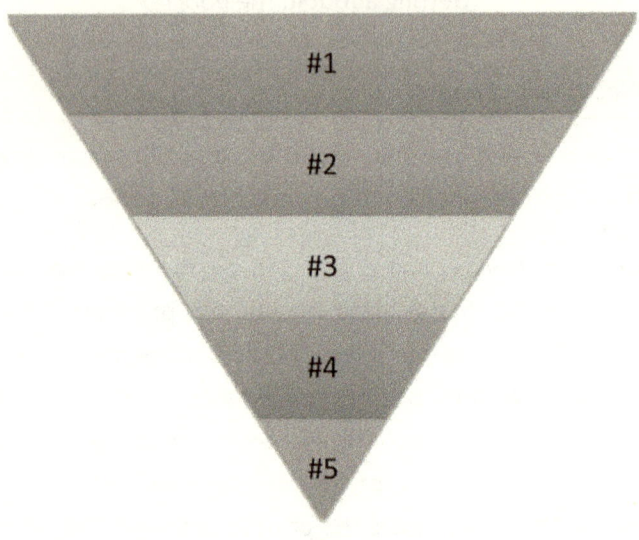

Where can you do the following?

1. Networking

2. Internships

3. Volunteering

4. Related Jobs

5. other

Where is your opportunity to gain exposure and relationships?

Timeline of Accomplishments

(Long term and short term goals)

Think about 5 separate ultimate goals within categories of family, career or life. Prioritize them from #1 to #5. Now you will elaborate on goal #1 of each, as they are broken down into short term and long term goals on the following page. Notice that People, Tools and Action Surround the goals.

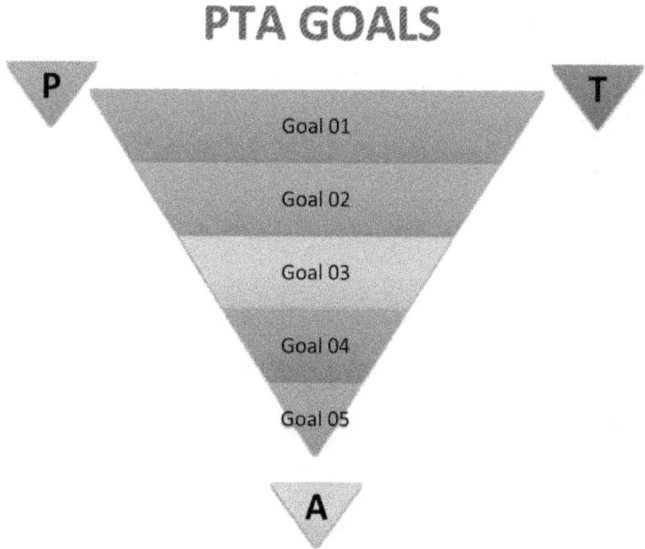

Priority goal #1 within each category (family, career life) – Ultimate Goals

Finding Purpose

Now, think about your short-term and long-term goals that lead up to your Ultimate Goal. Document in detail below what you will accomplish within the time period listed for each.

- *Family*
- *Career*
- *Life*

Family Short Term Goals:

> 1 month:
>
> 3 month:
>
> 6 month:
>
> 1 year:

Family Long Term Goals:

> 5 years

Career Short Term Goals:

> 1 month:
>
> 3 month:
>
> 6 month:
>
> 1 year:

Finding Purpose

Career Long Term Goals:

> 5 years

Life Short Term Goals:

> 1 month:
>
> 3 month:
>
> 6 month:
>
> 1 year:

Life Long Term Goals:

> 5 years

Ultimate Goal: Summarize your combined goal of family, career and life.

Finding Purpose

When someone says they will accomplish something, ask them what day it would be accomplished. People who will really accomplish something will have an anticipated date of completion.

BUILD YOUR PURPOSE

(Action Steps)
Power

What can we do right now to start building?

One of the most difficult parts of fulfilling a purpose is actually putting your actions into practice. It is true that in some cases, I have found people expressing why it is difficult to put action into place is because they're looking for perfection in their plan, or they are seeking validation. While this can many times be the case, typically speaking, the purpose that we pursue is usually connected to the vision of our lives that is given directly to us.

We cannot expect others to see the vision that has been cast for our lives in the same ways that we can. Each of us is an individual and each of us receives our visions in our own special ways. Waiting for someone to validate our actions toward our purpose is like waiting for someone else to receive the vision that we have for ourselves, which doesn't make a lot of sense at all.

Sometimes you can be moved to question whether you're qualified enough to accomplish your goal. This happens often, particularly when people are led to question their own credentials or the influence they have on others before deciding to take a specific action.

Be under no illusion - you are your credentials. Your credentials include your personal life experiences, both informal and formal, and anything else that has contributed to the decisions that inform your methods for taking action. The nature of your credentials can fall under many categories, such as spiritual, scientific, psychological, or social. But whatever your credentials may be, it is not always your responsibility to explain to others why or how you are qualified to fulfill your purpose.

Action steps: What's in my power at this moment to start building my dream?

Finding Purpose

"Have You Started" checklist:

- ☐ Making a plan
- ☐ Writing it down on paper
- ☐ Contacting people
- ☐ Seeking resources
- ☐ Visited related environment
- ☐ Volunteering/Internship
- ☐ Resume if needed
- ☐ Reading/Videos on the topic

Family: What will be your action steps towards your goals?

> 1 month:
>
> 3 month:
>
> 6 month:

Career: What will be your action steps towards your goals?

> 1 month:
>
> 3 month:
>
> 6 month:

Finding Purpose

Life: What will be your action steps towards your goals?

> 1 month:
>
> 3 month:
>
> 6 month:

What can you do today to begin working towards your goals?

Prioritization Chart – Action

Here you have laid out action steps. Thinking about your action steps within your 1 month (family, career, life) document 5 action steps that you can make within the first month, in order of priority.

Finding Purpose

Action

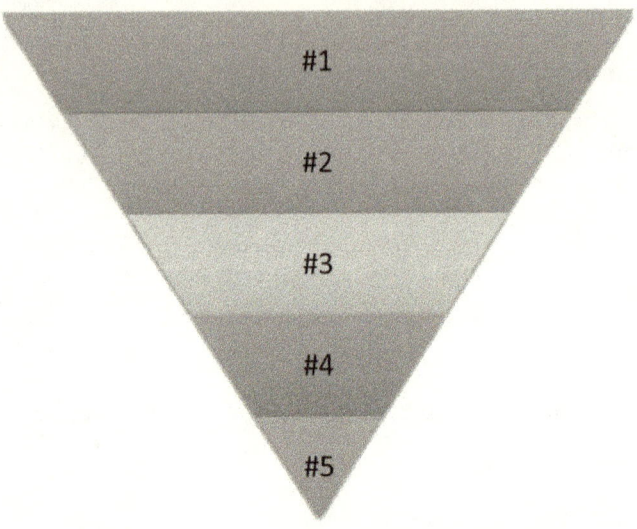

5 action steps within 1 month in order of priority. (Family, Career and/or Life).

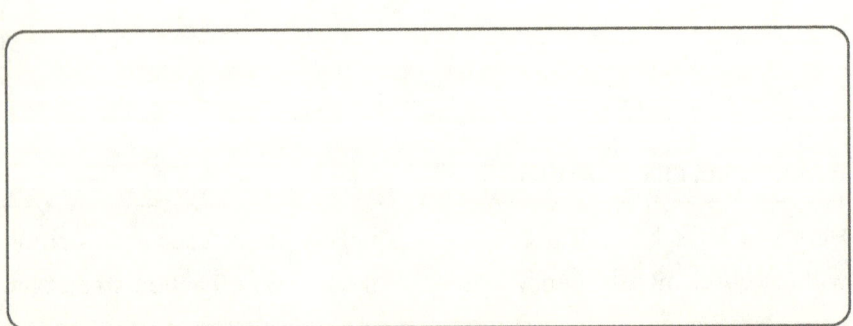

Finding Purpose

LIVE IN PURPOSE

(Perseverance, Endurance, Patience)
Dare to be Different

What will it take to live in Purpose?

Ways of dealing with stress: (mark what you will use)

- ☐ Meditation
- ☐ Prayer
- ☐ Focus
- ☐ Recreation
- ☐ Health and Nutrition
- ☐ Resting
- ☐ The proper amount of sleep
- ☐ Games
- ☐ Communicating
- ☐ Art
- ☐ Music
- ☐ Other

Ways of building endurance and perseverance:

- ☐ Working smart
- ☐ Working hard
- ☐ Accomplish something every day
- ☐ Finding inspiration
- ☐ Connecting to a mentor
- ☐ Have motivating friends
- ☐ Include Dream in a created daily schedule
- ☐ Thinking Positive
- ☐ Other

Finding Purpose

Write what it will require to build perseverance, endurance and patience:

Our Purpose is the crossing path between our passion and goals which typically touches our desires and conviction of responsibilities regarding our family, careers and our general lives. Review the documented responses and continue to identify the crossing paths to continue solidifying your purpose.

Finding Purpose

MAINTAIN

Civilization

How will you maintain your accomplishments?

Making productive decisions in life:

Dig deep to Find the **"Jewel"** within you -

When someone says you can't, **Hope** *is within you*

When someone makes you upset, **Peace** *is within you*

When someone turns their back, **Joy** *is within you*

When going through hard times, **Serenity** *is within you*

When what you want takes a long time to gain, **Patience** *is within you*

When you get tired, **Perseverance** *is within you*

When it's time to focus, **Knowledge** *is within you*

When a decision needs to be made, **Wisdom** *is within you*

When you are frustrated, **Kindness** *is within you*

When someone makes a mistake, **Understanding** *is within you*

When you stay grounded, **Success** *is revealed from you*

To keep what we earn, we must respond to every situation in a civilized fashion, by depending on the qualities within us, when making decisions. Utilizing your qualities will allow you to overcome your circumstances.

If you agree to depend on your Qualities, please sign below:

Signature

SELF-DEFEATING LABELS

These are names many people call themselves when feeling down. We can feel various ways below, without attaching the label to us. Identify any labels that sound familiar, so that you can become more aware of them as influences of self-defeat.

loser	awkward
lazy	helpless
stupid	incapable
selfish	inferior
ugly	fraud
criminal	unlovable
addict	outcast
fat	boring
weak	loner
worthless	mediocre
boring	quiet
emotional	loud
hyper	bad
crazy	strange
psycho	incompetent
nerd	failure
weird	lazy
lousy	ineffective
unlikeable odd	senseless
unattractive	unskilled
shy	worthless
insignificant	gullible

Finding Purpose

Positive Self-Affirming Words

Review the affirming words below and choose which qualities you hold. Once you choose the qualities, describe how they are or will be exhibited in your life.

- Accomplished
- Accountable
- Adaptable
- Ambitious
- Analytical
- Articulate
- Assertive
- Attentive
- Authentic
- Balanced
- Brave
- Calm
- Candid
- Capable
- Careful
- Cheerful
- Collaborative
- Committed
- Determined
- Diligent
- Discerning
- Driven
- Dynamic
- Easygoing
- Efficient
- Encouraging
- Energetic
- Entrepreneurial
- Ethical
- Experienced
- Fair
- Fearless
- Flexible
- Friendly
- Genuine
- Goal-oriented
- Observant
- Open-minded
- Optimistic
- Particular
- Passionate
- Patient
- Perseverant
- Persistent
- Personable
- Persuasive
- Positive
- Practical
- Precise
- Proactive
- Productive
- Rational
- Reliable
- Respectful

Finding Purpose

- Communicative
- Compassionate
- Confident
- Conscientious
- Consistent
- Constructive
- Cooperative
- Courageous
- Creative
- Cultured
- Curious
- Daring
- Decisive
- Dedicated
- Dependable
- Hardworking
- Honest
- Imaginative
- Independent
- Innovative
- Integrity
- Knowledgeable
- Leader
- Level-headed
- Loyal
- Mature
- Mediator
- Mindful
- Motivated
- Objective
- Responsible
- Self-disciplined
- Sensible
- Skilled
- Spiritual
- Strategic
- Successful
- Tactful
- Thorough
- Trustworthy
- Understanding
- Unique
- Versatile
- Visionary

ENJOYING THE BENEFITS

(Responsibility, Contributing to Society)

The most successful people in the world have figured out that when you give back to Society/Humanity/Community, you do not only get the satisfaction of contributing, but somehow their success usually grows.

Contributions/Causes -

While you are living in your Purpose, what and how will you contribute to Mankind?

[ ]

Balance -

It is important that we take time to meditate in order to connect with deeper parts of ourselves and clear our minds of the everyday stresses that can keep us occupied. We must apply serenity and balance to our lives so that we don't become overwhelmed with the consumption of responsibilities that may seem to never end. You are worthy to celebrate your victories of your purpose.

Celebrate -

What does celebrating a victory look like to you? When you are celebrating, are you expecting to receive a tangible award, such as a plaque or trophy? Rather you desire something tangible or not, there is nothing wrong with you creating that plaque or trophy for yourself. You can even create a certificate, print it out, and sign it, all with the purpose of acknowledging yourself. Monumentalizing a moment requires no

Finding Purpose

necessary authorization from someone else on the outside. You can validate your own accomplishments and be proud the same way that other people can.

Finding Purpose Affirmation

I am here by design, not default. I am here to fulfill a purpose. My qualities are unique therefore, I am the only one who can give what I have to offer this world. I have unlimited possibilities, I was not created to be placed in a box, I was not created to be defined by class, status, or the opinions of those around me. I am defined by the positive traits within me. I am the only person who has lived my life; therefore, I am the only one who can fulfill my purpose in life. The greatest thing that I have to offer to this world, is me.

WHAT'S NEEDED

TO TURN A DREAM INTO REALITY?

TO LIVE A PURPOSEFUL LIFE

FIELD TRIP

(Take a Trip)

It's like telling someone you're going to love pizza, but they've never had pizza. So, they don't even know what it tastes like, but once they taste it when they smell it or you talk about it, their mouth waters. So, visit a place that reminds you of or a place where you can experience living in your purpose. In hopes, the holistic experience of living on purpose becomes even more organic over time.

THE AUTHORS

Catherine Frenes has an extensive professional history of Real Estate and Business Management, and contributes her insight on spirituality, within this book of Finding Purpose.

Finding Purpose

Johnathan Kendrick possesses years of experience in business/non-profit management and development. During his career, he has worked with individuals and families, helping them stabilize by addressing barriers within their lives.

Finding Purpose

April Peebles is a proud, educated mother, professionally trained in hypnotherapy. She has also successfully partnered with organizations to help clients create positive changes mentally, physically, and spiritually, in their personal and professional lives.

Finding Purpose

Rob O' Brien is a Life Coach with Core Intention Coaching. He has successfully assisted clients with deepening their personal connection physically, mentally, and spiritually. He contributes practical insight into one's natural ability to connect with their purpose.

Finding Purpose

Adriana Soto is described as a testimony of change and exhibits an example of the possibilities that surpass expectations. She contributes a unique perspective on the power of love, in relation to its ability to transform lives.

Finding Purpose

Mary Tilton first fell in love with the social sciences when first introduced to Psychology, Sociology, and Speech classes. After studying them for a few years in college, she eventually became a hairstylist and is able to continue to see them play out every day. She is a mother, sister, friend, daughter, harmless inquisitor, wandering soul, and a perpetually positive person.

www.ingramcontent.com/pod-product-compliance
Lightning Source LLC
Chambersburg PA
CBHW051650040426
42446CB00009B/1059